# Blogging For Beginners

By Salvador Briggman

Copyright © 2018 Salvador Briggman LLC

All rights reserved. No part of this publication may be reproduced, distributed, or transmitted in any form or by any means, including photocopying, recording, or other electronic or mechanical methods, without the prior written permission of the publisher, except in the case of brief quotations embodied in critical reviews and certain other noncommercial uses permitted by copyright law.

Although the author and publisher have made every effort to ensure that the information in this book was correct at press time, the author and publisher do not assume and hereby disclaim any liability to any party for any loss, damage, or disruption caused by errors or omissions, whether such errors or omissions result from negligence, accident, or any other cause.

The book is not intended for use as a source of legal or financial advice. You should always consult legal and financial professionals to provide specific guidance in evaluating and pursing investment or business opportunities. The advice, examples, and strategies in this book are not suitable for every situation. The materials are not intended to represent or guarantee desired results.

http://www.salvadorbriggman.com

# Introduction

It was literally insane. I was 24 years old, and I felt like I was rich. I could go anywhere, at any time, and had no one to answer to. At a moment's notice, I could book a trip to Brazil, Spain, South Africa, or France. What's more... I'd make money while I was traveling.

The catch was, I wasn't rich. Nowhere close. Don't get me wrong, I was making good money. I was living in New York City. I could afford to party, eat out, and even save money. But, my **time** wasn't tied to my money. I was making money in my sleep, and not even trying.

Sounds like the story behind some kind of scam, right? I thought so too.

I never bought into book titles like "The Four-Hour Work Week," "Rich Dad Poor Dad," or "Think and Grow Rich."

I thought they were scammy marketers trying to sell poor saps the dream of getting rich quickly. Real results take decades to achieve and only come at the price of ignoring your friends, family, and lover, right?

Why then was *I* the exception? Why was it that I was **thriving** when many of the people I went to school with were struggling to get by in a competitive job marketplace?

When I talked about my job with relatives and family members, they'd raise their eyebrows in surprise. They'd look at me doubtfully and say, "And you can make money at that?"

Of course I could! After all, so many people online were making a killing. In fact, one of the friends that I grew up with was making lots of money with a website that ranked Minecraft servers. This site was getting millions of views a month and here's the catch... he was younger than me.

What I was doing online seemed completely obvious. Anyone could do it. But, when I explained it, I would always get blank stares.

People couldn't comprehend the fact that I was able to set up a blog so easily and rake in cash, even when I was sleeping. I had to be lying or doing something illegal. Otherwise, everyone would be doing it!

After several years, I came to fully understand why my existence was so foreign to them. I finally got why it didn't make sense and never would make sense. I'll sum it up for you in one simple formula.

Average Beliefs + Average Actions + Average Commitment = Average Results.

According to the Bureau of Labor Statistics average individual in the United States bringing home about $49,400 per year from age 34 – 44. That's a standard 9 - 5 job where you're working 40 hours per week! I made more money than that my second-year of blogging, and I didn't have to work all that much either.

If you want to succeed in a way that other people aren't, you have to go outside of the mainstream. You can't just follow the system, like everyone else. You need empowering beliefs, mentors, and a high level of commitment towards your dream. You gotta get outside your comfort zone.

It might seem weird at first, but you must be willing to explore different ways of thinking about the world. You have to take actions that the "mainstream" considers risky.

In life, you can either develop a plan for your own life, or have other people develop a plan for you. You'll quickly become a pillar building **their** dream, rather than your own.

Just think, how are you spending your time each day?

Are you managing other people, and organizing them towards your goals? Or, are *you* the one being managed?

Our social conditioning in our society is focused on two things.

1. Making us great consumers.

2. Making us great employees.

Don't believe me? You better listen up.

Every single emotion that you feel on a daily basis guides your purchasing behaviors. Marketers, like myself, are very aware of this. It's one reason that we promote stories, values, and lifestyles that are meant to stir up emotions that will eventually lead to a purchasing decision.

What do young girls do when they realize the "importance" of beauty, popularity, and boys?

They go out and buy makeup. They buy expensive clothes and jewelry. They attempt to look desirable to the opposite sex and they seek approval from the same sex. The majority of women out there are not comfortable with their looks. Why do you think eating disorders are so prevalent? These negative emotions are riled up by marketers and our own social conditioning in order to turn us into obedient consumers.

Think about it... as young men, we're sold stories like the Wolf of Wall Street, Pretty Woman, and The Social Network that make us want to go out there earn a lot of money. With money, we can *finally* win the attention of girls and gain respect from our peers. We'll even be able to party it up, because that's what you do in your 20s, and of course, that's what you need to do to get laid.

This negative mentality fuels the consumption of alcohol, expensive goods, and oddly enough, it creates hard working employees. I'm *not* saying that this is all a conspiracy. I'm just saying that this is how our society operates.

Let's take music as an example. So many of the popular rap songs and mainstream music pieces talk about going out, hitting up chicks or chasing boys, and getting drunk in the club. Just look at the lyrics of Time of Our Lives by Pitbull.

"I knew my rent was gon' be later 'bout a week ago

I work my ass off

But I still can't pay it though

But I got just enough

To get up in this club

Have me a good time, before my time is up

Hey, let's get it now."

Haha! If I owned a club, I'd play that song all the time. Young guys who barely have enough money to pay rent will spend their cash trying to buy a hot girl a drink and a shot for themselves, because they gotta party it up!!

This is just one example of how our culture promotes consumption. There are countless others. Marketers prey on negative emotions, promote stories, and sell lifestyles that will result in a thriving consumer base.

Our social conditioning also trains us to be great employees. From a very young age, we are taught in school to be good at key skills that have little real practicality when it comes to actual business or financial management. When is the last time that you used geometry, trigonometry, calculus, or applied your knowledge about ancient Victorian literature? Chances are, it's been a while.

I'm not saying that these topics don't have value. I actually love literature and stories. I'm just saying that the education system is set up to churn out employees, not business owners.

Think about it... what do schools and colleges prize?

They brag about standardized test scores, ivy league acceptances, employment rates, kids who got into their first-choice college, and of course, they emphasize getting **as much** education as possible. Don't worry about student loans. Go and get that graduate degree in ancient Chinese philosophy.

Want to set up a business? Go and get an MBA!

Need to make more money? Get a PhD!

We're taught that higher education equates to more money. When we get that money, we can then go out and buy happiness with that big flat screen TV with "same as cash" financing that only requires a low monthly payment.

All the while, you're making expensive private colleges money, you're making the TV business rich, and you're making bankers wealthy with your "low" monthly payments. Who's really getting the best deal out of this situation?

What makes this all even more absurd is that college tuition is at a record high. We're paying more for college degrees than ever before in history. Couple that fact with easy student loan financing and it's a recipe for a bubble. The funny thing is that this entire system is *justified* by the fact that you're going to get a high paying job after college. Good joke, right?

When you imagine all of the forces conspiring to keep you living a plain life as a thoughtless consumer and obedient employee, it can seem hopeless. It's like this massive tidal wave that you're powerless to stop. Soon, you'll surrender to its power and be carried down into the depths of the cold, heartless ocean.

I'm happy to tell you that that doesn't have to happen. You can break free from this system and I can show you exactly how to do it.

It's not going to be easy. You're going to have to read **every** word of this entire book, take **massive** action, and adopt a completely **new** mindset. But, if you do, you'll finally gain that sense of financial and emotional freedom that I too have always craved.

This book is going to show you exactly how to **start your own blog** and turn it into a *full-time cash-generating machine.* I'm going to give you the keys to the kingdom, which will unlock this entirely new career that you never thought possible.

You'll quickly discover how to get traffic, subscribers, readers, and build up passive income streams. I'll even share with you the most ***profitable*** niches online today and how you can get a slice of the pie.

While I'm gonna help you get your career on track, this book is about much more than just your job (or even your passion). It's about freedom. The ability to do what you want, when you want, without a boss lingering over your shoulder.

It's the freedom that comes with being able to take "mini-retirements" and spend months in a foreign country. It's the freedom you'll feel when you don't have to depend on a paycheck to be able to feed your family.

If you are a mother, a father, or just looking to contribute to your family, you'll also find that blogging is a great way to bring in extra income from the comfort of your home.

My name's Sal. I wrote this book and I can't wait for you to get started! Good luck!

- Sal

P.S. Don't forget to drop me a line and share **YOUR** story. (http://www.salvadorbriggman.com/contact)

*"People don't want to be millionaires — they want to experience what they believe only millions can buy."* - **Timothy Ferriss**

# Table of Contents

| | |
|---|---|
| Chapter 1: How to Make Money Blogging | 1 |
| Chapter 2: How Much Money Can You Make Blogging? | 25 |
| Chapter 3: How to Start a Blog | 32 |
| Chapter 4: Write Killer Blog Posts | 42 |
| Chapter 5: How to Get A River of Traffic to Your Blog | 55 |
| Chapter 6: How to Attract Raving Fans and Loyal Readers | 70 |
| Chapter 7: A Blogging Success Story... | 83 |
| Chapter 8: Passive Income and The Laptop Lifestyle | 89 |
| Chapter 9: Conclusion | 100 |

# Chapter 1: How to Make Money Blogging

I wasn't always a "full-time blogger" as they say. When I launched my first serious blog, I was a junior in college at George Washington University.

It was a frigid fall day. Thanksgiving was just around the corner. I was crammed, working at a tiny desk in my even tinier dorm room.

As I worked at my laptop, every so often, I'd curse and cross off a line on my quickly shrinking list of potential blog "domain names." A few hours ago, I had so many bright ideas. Now, it seemed like they were ALL taken.

My girlfriend was laying patiently on my bed, looking through her phone messages. In her one hand, she twirled a strand of straight brown hair between her delicate fingers. In the other, she scrolled past a mix of emails from her sorority, college, and part-time job at the campus gym.

"When do you want to head to the party?" She asked.

I turned, "Give me another 15 and we can go."

I don't remember much, but I do remember the greasy taste of a $0.99 7-Eleven pizza slice. I know, right? Yuck!

But, I lived just around the corner from one those convenience stores, and you can't beat that price. At the time, I didn't have any kind of income to speak of, let alone money to eat out.

Looking back, I can't help but laughing. I had absolutely no idea what I was doing. I read somewhere online that you can "make money blogging," and I decided to try it out and see what happened. After all, what did I have to lose?

The idea sounded kind of ludicrous. How can you actually earn an income by publishing blog posts online?

My parents always warned me against the idea of "quick riches" or promises that were "too good to be true." As you might imagine, I was very skeptical. I had my doubts.

Deep in my heart, I knew that I didn't NEED to be rich. If I could make even a fraction of what some of the top bloggers were pulling in, I'd be more than happy.

Up until that time in my life, I'd been told what to do by bosses and teachers. I'd been following an academic career track that was supposed to lead me to "success", only it wasn't.

I wasn't happy. Actually, that's an understatement. I was MISERABLE.

"Cha-ching!"

My girlfriend looked over at me.

"I got it! This is it!"

I pushed back from the desk and stood up proudly.

"CrowdCrux... dot com."

She looked kind of confused.

"Can you elaborate?" she asked.

"Well.. crowd for crowdfunding and crux for ... like... a hub. The center of. It will be an educational resource for crowdfunding."

She smiled and kissed me on the cheek.

At the time, no one knew what crowdfunding was. Heck, I only had an elementary grasp of it. I was doing a mini-economic thesis on Kickstarter, and naturally, it was required research.

Little did I know that within a year, this tiny, minute decision to finally "launch" a blog would lead to millions of website visitors, thousands of social media followers, a heck of a lot of subscribers, and a thriving career as a blogger.

Since that time, I've been cited by major media publications like Forbes, The New York Times, The Wall Street Journal, CNN, and more. I've been invited to speak all over the world and I've even given talks at NYU events and the Harvard Kennedy School of Government.

Great things start small. None of us have everything figured out. I had to learn as I went, and I made a ton of mistakes along the way.

It started with humble beginnings. I didn't have any money. I had zero blogging skills. I didn't know how to get traffic to my website or grow my subscribers.

Let me ask... does this sound like YOU?

Are you working to launch, grow, or monetize your blog?

Then, this book is **perfect** for you. Why? Because I'm just like you. I hate it when people don't give you a straight answer.

They'll beat around the bush, talk about a bunch of different things, and change the topic of the conversation. It's like... they're running for political office or something.

I'm not like that. I'm the real deal. And, I'm going to let you in on a little secret.

This is the real reason that bloggers (like me) are able to earn a full-time income from their website.

By the end of this chapter, you'll have an "aha" moment and a much clearer understanding of how this whole blogging business works.

I'm embarrassed to admit that I didn't fully understand this concept when I got started. It lead to a lot of frustration and anxiety. Why was it that my income wasn't going up, and up?

On the outside, it seemed like I was doing everything right. I was getting more traffic and more subscribers. But, little did I know that the "engine" I built had a fatal flaw.

I was focusing on the wrong metrics.

Before I share this "revelation" that I had, let me tell you a little story. Months before I graduated college I was offered a job working at a great startup company in Washington, DC.

My starting salary was gonna be a little over $50,000.

It was in a terrific area of the city. The team seemed young, hungry, and motivated.

But, to the surprise of my friends, parents, and teachers, I turned down that job.

I had made up my mind that I wanted to build **my own** company after college. This was my one shot. I was going to do **whatever it took** and work however many hours I needed in order to be successful.

At graduation, I got to celebrate the ending of my college years with my relatives and friends. Of course, everyone asked what I was going to do after college and I told them. I was going to start a new company.

I got lots of polite smiles and nervous laughter. Don't get me wrong, everyone I talked to was very nice, but deep down I could tell that no one really believed that I could do it. To tell you the truth, I'm not sure if I believed myself. I knew that I would only be serious about this decision if I totally committed to it. So, a few months after graduation, I moved to NYC with one month's rent to my name and started grinding away.

I share this story with you because I'm just like you. I didn't have much money when I was getting started. I had zero blogging experience and I didn't know anything about online business. I was scared, nervous, and excited all at once.

Flash forward two years later and all the hard work paid off. I earned **$50k** that year directly from my blog. Wow!

That was more money that I had ever earned in my lifetime, and I did it from the comfort of my own home. In my mind, I had made it. I was living the laptop lifestyle. I could go and travel any time I wanted. I could work however much or little I wanted. I was my own boss.

Now... I know there are some bloggers out there earning millions of dollar per year with their blog. I'm not one of those (at least, not yet).

I can't show you how to get rich, but I can show you exactly how to earn a healthy income doing work that you love. The first step is to change your view of what blogging is. You've been sold a lie, and it's time to tell you the truth.

**The Blog is a "Lead Magnet" not a "Product"**

A blog isn't a *business*.

A blog is simply a collection of FREE content on a particular subject.

If you produce high quality blog posts, then this free content will attract regular visitors to your website. Once a visitor is on your website, that's where the fun begins!

A funny thing happens when someone around the world reads your content. They **get to know you** a little bit better. When you help them with some aspect of their business or life, they're far more likely to trust you, and as a result, do business with you.

Fundamentally, a blog is a lead magnet. You're using to create a bunch of leads that you can sell products or services to down the road. You can also sell other people's products and services to this audience by way of sponsored posts, affiliate marketing, and advertisements.

If you were to ask an established agency how they viewed blogging, they would tell you it's "inbound marketing" or "content marketing." This is just fancy terminology for "you use it to turn traffic into prospects and prospects into customers."

**Bloggers Don't Rely on One Pay Check**

When you work for an employer, you have ONE income stream. Your paycheck.

As a blogger, you're going to need to build up multiple income streams if you want to earn a healthy amount from blogging.

This could include:

- Coaching and consulting
- Freelancing
- Services
- Advertisements
- Sponsorships
- Ebooks and Audio Books

- Online courses
- In-person events
- Membership websites
- Physical products
- Affiliate marketing

I'm not going to cover every single way that you can earn income in this book, but I do want to hit a few of the major revenue sources for most bloggers. No matter what you do for your day job, keep an open mind as you're reading the next section. You never know how your career will change or transform!

**Freelancing**

By far, freelancing is the easiest way to make money online and, by hiring freelancers and selling the services of your own contractors, you can even create an agency or service-based business.

Creating a successful business really comes down to your own skills and the skills of those that you can hire. You can get an idea of the type of skills that are in demand by browsing marketplaces like:

- Elance
- Upwork
- Freelancer

In order to begin an online service-based business, you're going to need:

- Customer testimonials
- Previous projects you've work on

- A good-looking website/blog
- A way to bill customers, track the progress of projects, and communication tools
- A marketing plan

Remember, most customer will be discovering you by reading your blog articles! The blog will introduce prospects to your writing skills and expertise. This will make it a heck of a lot easier to get them to hire you.

Here are some ideas for a service-based online company:

- Writing service
- Social media marketing
- Custom video or audio work
- Transcription
- Virtual assistant

Again, it comes down to your skills and the skills of the people you hire.

**Digital Products and Courses**

In the last 5 years, new software has made it really easy to put together digital products and sell them online. These could include products like:

- Ebooks
- Video courses
- Audio books
- Templates and blueprints
- Software extensions (plugins, themes, etc).

Before I talk about eBooks, physical books, and guides, let me just say that it's scary to ask people to actually pay money for something that you've created.

An easy way to begin to work up the courage to charge for a higher priced product, like a course, it to begin with eBooks. When you host the ebook on your own website, you can charge anywhere from $10 – $30. You might even be able to charge more if the content is very sought after.

If you're publishing the book on Amazon, you'll probably be pricing the ebook at $2.99 and the physical book between $6 – $10. Amazon will then take a fee and distribute you royalties.

There are a lot of tools that you can use to deliver this ebook to website visitors, including:

- Gumroad
- OptimizePress + PayPal
- Digital Downloads Plugin

You're not going to make a tremendous amount from ebooks. However, it will prove to you that:

1. Yes, you can sell a digital product online
2. Yes, people will be happy they paid for it.

You'll begin to gain more confidence knowing that you can actually sell products through your blog to your readers. It's also pretty sweet that you'll be generating a passive income stream.

Once you create the ebook or physical book, you don't have to make another. You can just sell copies, and you don't even have to be there for the transaction to take place, hence the passive income.

If you're looking for inspiration, check out the Amazon marketplace and the best seller list in various categories.

Also, be sure to read all of the negative reviews. They can give clues as to what people WANT to learn but didn't find in this book.

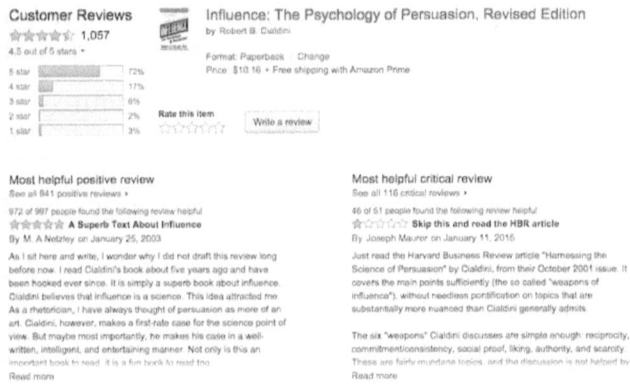

Aside from ebooks, you can also look into online courses. In the last several years, online courses have grown into a massive revenue stream for many bloggers out there. Personally, they've contributed a lot to the growth of my income.

Online courses go hand and hand with blogging. Most bloggers that I know are teachers. They're educating a particular niche about a specific topic. They're helping them answer questions and solve problems.

When you take this approach, ebooks, consulting, and online courses are a complete no brainer. They are more ways that a blogger can help educate and teach readers. The reason that online courses are so powerful is that, like an ebook, you can create it once and sell it many times. This is the formula for ongoing passive income!

Simply put, online courses are scalable and what's more, they command a high price point. While you have to sell 20 ebooks per month at the $20 price point to make $400, you only need to sell one or two courses.

With a high price point, you can also afford to advertise the course on social media networks like Facebook. This will bring in new students and allow you to advertise even more. Cool, eh?

I foresee online courses becoming a major source of income for myself and other bloggers in the next 5-10 years. It's where the action is at! There are many software tools that you can use to create an online course. Here are a list of tools you can use:

- Thinkific
- Teachable
- OptimizePress
- Udemy

To get an idea of the courses that are already out there, you can browse online marketplaces like Udemy or Lynda.

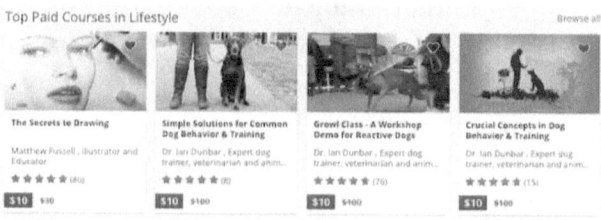

## Banner Advertisements

It doesn't seem like it, but banner advertisements actually still make money. I still generate a significant income stream from advertisements in the form of Google's Adsense Program and BuySellAds.

The great thing about advertisements is that they're passive income. You're selling the attention of your blog visitors and readers to a 3rd party. Typically, this is a company that's interested in reaching those readers. While you probably won't get rich from banner ads, they are an easy way to begin to generate some cash in the early stages.

I fondly remember earning my very first $2 from Adsense in 2012. I was able to take my girlfriend out to coffee – haha!

For me, Adsense was a great motivational tool. It proved to me that I could make money from blogging. I just had to generate more traffic.

Seeing my earning going up made me want to write EVEN MORE high-quality articles and get them out there as fast as possible.

I had never experienced anything like it. Advertisers were actually paying to be shown on my blog. This wasn't Monopoly money. This was cold hard cash.

Google Adsense is a marketplace. Advertisers compete and bid for advertising inventory. If there's more competition, the cost per click goes up. If there's less competition, the price goes down. Why does this matter?

If you're writing about a popular topic and advertisers want to reach your audience, they're going to be competing with each other and end up driving the cost per click price up, making you more money.

If you're writing about a topic that no one cares about, and advertisers don't have any interest in reaching your audience, then they're going to experience very low cost per clicks and you'll make less revenue.

Therefore, if you're trying to maximize your income from Adsense, it makes sense to write about topics that attract audiences that advertisers are willing to pay to reach.

### Sponsored Content

Sponsored articles are another easy way to begin to earn some income as you're getting started as a blogger. They're an important income stream, just don't oversaturate your readers.

With a sponsored article, a 3rd party company is basically saying that they want to reach your blog readers in a more engaged way than a banner advertisement.

They might have you write the article or they might provide their own article for you to publish on your blog. Not only will this give them access to your readership, but it also gives them a back link, which is powerful in the eyes of Google.

Technically, you should always "nofollow" your back links for sponsored posts, but not every blogger does that. While you can earn healthy money by taking offers for sponsored content, don't compromise your values!

Your relationship with your readers should always be your highest priority. Otherwise, they're going to smell that you're money-hungry and they won't take your recommendations as seriously.

### Social Media and Advertising Packages

As you begin to grow your blog, you'll come to find that your audience will spill over across multiple social networks and other channels, like an email subscriber list.

At this point in time, you should think of yourself as a small media company. Media companies don't only make money from banner ads. They also sell advertising packages.

Your advertising package could take the form of:

- Social media promotion
- Banner ads
- Email list blast
- Sponsored content, etc.

Creating an advertising package will naturally allow you to command a higher rate. You'll also give advertisers maximum exposure to your readership.

**Live Events and Online Summits**

Hosting live events are another great way to monetize the audience that you've built up. You can sell tickets to a conference or even an online summit where you'll be going more in-depth into your subject matter.

Live training can command a very high price point and create some great social proof for your brand in the way of photos and videos. It will also give you the opportunity to form deeper one-on-once connections with your readers.

One of the big benefits of holding a live event or online summit is that you can also bring in other voices to teach your readers about a particular subject. You'll be able to network with other experts in your community and grow your brand alongside theirs.

**Mastermind Groups**

Lastly, a growing income stream that I've noticed, particularly for big-name bloggers is the concept of ultra exclusive mastermind groups.

A mastermind group is designed to forward the business goals of the members also form tight knit connections among the participants.

Premium mastermind groups typically will charge members to become a part of the group. A simple example of this is Lewis Howe's Summit of Greatness.

Of course, in order to create this income stream, you're going to need to have been blogging in your niche for a while. Usually members of the mastermind will be readers who have gotten results from your teachings and want to take it to the next level.

You'll also need the connections with other high profile influencers to persuade readers of the value of joining your exclusive mastermind group.

**Consulting and Coaching**

In the early days, this is how most bloggers earn an income. They'll offer consulting, coaching or business services to their readers.

You might think... why would ANYONE pay me money for my advice?

Good question! The main reason is that when you write a comprehensive article, you demonstrate your knowledge on a particular topic.

It shows people that you know what you're talking about. It also gives them a chance to get to know you a little. This makes strangers more comfortable hiring you to help them with their business or life.

But, this shouldn't surprise you. This is why many authors write books. They want those high-priced speaking and consulting gigs. They want to solidify themselves as an "expert" on a particular topic.

You can begin to earn income by using your blog a secret weapon for generating leads that will pay you for your time.

## Affiliate Marketing And Selling Other People's Products

Affiliate marketing is another important income stream for my blog business. It's something that I started to get involved in after the first year or so of blogging.

The concept behind affiliate marketing is simple. Rather than creating your own digital or physical products, you can sell OTHER PEOPLE's products.

You'll then get a commission when you sell one of these products.

Now, in order to make decent money from affiliate marketing, you're going to need an audience that you can broadcast these offers to either via email or linking to the products in your blog post. This is why most beginners don't start here.

Aside from online courses, which I'll get into later, affiliate marketing is the closest thing I've come to in terms of "magic money."

You can have income distributed into your bank account without even doing anything. The other company takes care of all of the customer service. You just collect commission checks.

It's pretty freaking sweet. It's also 100% passive income.

I have blog posts that I've written years ago that still earn me income.

If you're ready to hit the ground running, take a look into these affiliate programs:

- Commission Junction

- Impact Radius
- Clickbank
- Rakuten
- ShareaSale
- Amazon

These are broad affiliate programs where most people can find products to sell. There are also niche-specific affiliate programs. You can even hash out a deal with a company in your niche, as I have, to earn commission when you refer customers.

I know that the allure of money is enticing for a bootstrapped blogger, but again, don't compromise your vales. You'll regret it later. Don't sell shitty products.

**The Types of Blogs that Make Good Money**

Certain blog niches and topics are proven to make more money than others.

Why?

Simple! Supply and demand.

There are a definitive number of human beings searching out key topics on Google, Facebook, etc. They are looking for:

- Educational information
- Entertaining distractions
- News alerts
- Solutions to their problems

Now, if you want don't start a blog in one of the "main niches" that I'm going to mention, don't fret. After all, my very first professional blog was about crowdfunding, which is a niche topic.

However, you WILL find that almost every profitable micro-niche usually tends to fall under one of these categories. For example, I would put "crowdfunding" under the "business advice" category.

Make sense?

These are some of the types of blogs that make good money...

**Fashion and Beauty**

This category has always existed, will always exist, and if you have an audience, can be ridiculously profitable. When I say "fashion and beauty" I'm referring to tips on what to wear, how to wear it, makeup, and everything that goes into how you portray yourself to the world.

Naturally, this niche is very popular for females, but there are also some guys out there that are killing it. Many have sizable followings on Instagram, Facebook, or YouTube.

The reason this category is profitable is because there are a ton of ways to monetize your blog. You can recommend products, do sponsored content, sell your own lines, and more.

People will always want to look good, so this niche isn't going away anytime.

Examples include:

- MyFashDiary
- Fishnets and Rainbows
- The Blonde Salad
- Song of Style
- Gal Meet Glam

**Personal Finance**

This is another evergreen topic that always has demand. Just look at all the books out there on personal finance. Everything that has to do with saving, investing, and managing your money can be lumped into this category.

A lot of these blogs will talk about how to get out of debt, invest for retirement, save effectively, and get better deals. There are many companies, products, and services out there that will help individuals do this, making it a profitable niche to go into.

Examples include:

- Get Rich Slowly
- The Simple Dollar
- Financial Samuri
- Making Cents of Cents
- Penny Hoarder

**Fitness and Healthy Living**

Fitness is a billion-dollar industry. There are tons of weight loss products, supplements, muscle building programs, and more. Naturally, there is also a large base of consumers interested in learning more about fitness and healthy living, hence the popular blog niche.

As this topic becomes more and more popular, we also see rising sub-topics like meditation and mental health.

Examples include:

- Nerd Fitness
- Workout Mommy
- Daily Burn

- Powercakes
- Lean Green Bean

**News and Politics**

People are curious about the world around them. They want to stay up to date on what's happening in the world. Of course, there are major news organizations out there that help satisfy this basic desire. However, there are a growing number of online commentators that provide their perspective on the news

In addition, there are many blogs that have sprung up that provide a specific point of view on the news (liberal, conservative, etc). With the rise of social media networks like Facebook, everyone is getting into the news business. For example, niche tech blogs are breaking real stories in the technology realm.

Years ago, this used to be reserved only for the major newspapers, and maybe some magazines.

Examples include:

- Huffington Post
- Mashable
- Business Insider
- Recode
- Crooks and Liars

**Make Money Online**

Aaaaand, of course there's the "make money online" industry.

There are tons of ways that you can make money online, including:

- Launching a blog

- Growing a podcast
- Starting a YouTube channel
- Drop shipping
- Selling on Amazon
- Affiliate marketing
- and much, much more.

I would actually lump the MMO industry under a "career" or "business" category. More often than not, people are searching out information on how to improve their income or get a better job.

If you've been successful in any of the categories on this blog post, you could theoretically talk about how to earn an income online. Therefore, it's a very saturated niche.

Examples include:

- EOFire
- Smart Passive Income
- Femtrepreneur
- Probloger
- Salvador Briggman

**Food**

If you haven't already, you should be noticing a trend. Many of these topics are also very popular when it comes to book categories. Food has been and always will be a popular category in the blogging world. There are many amateur chefs out there that want to learn new cooking skills.

In addition, I think it's fair to say that 99% of the world loves food. This is a topic that's always going to be in demand.

Examples include:

- Simply Recipes
- Orangette
- Smitten Kitchen
- David Lebovitz
- Not Without Salt

**DIY and Crafts**

With the growth of Etsy, Pinterest, and YouTube, we've seen the emergence of a whole slew of DIY and craft bloggers. Many of these types of blogs focus on interior design, life hacks, and re-modeling your home on a budget. We've also seen a lot of mommy bloggers transition into this niche.

Examples include:

- Addicted 2 Decorating
- Old Town Home
- The Design Confidential
- Manhattan Nest
- Remodelaholic

**Self-Improvement**

Self-improvement, personal development, or self-help all stand for one thing... helping people see a radical transformation in their life!

This could include:

- Emotional mastery
- Dating and relationships
- Cultivating Happiness
- Family
- and more.

Usually, blogs in this industry are focused on helping readers get in touch with who they really are, so that they can set corresponding goals and a compelling vision for the future.

Examples include:

- Life Hack
- Art of Manliness
- Addicted2Success
- Positivity Blog
- Four Hour Work Week

**Entertainment**

Lastly, the web has been a boom for entertaining content. Just look at all of the publications that have racked up views and advertising dollars from Facebook.

Many of these blogs have gotten "shock" and "awe" down to a formula. They get their traffic by promising and delivering on key emotions, such as:

- Humor
- Surprise
- Anger or Outrage

- Weird Things or Uniqueness

The key to a good entertainment blog is to be a master of crafting headlines, thumbnails, and knowing good content when you see it.

Example include:

- BuzzFeed
- Viral Nova
- Bored Panda
- Distractify

**Where Should You Get Started?**

As you can see, there are many ways to earn an income from blogging. If you're using the blog to teach about a particular subject, then I'd recommend starting out with coaching and services. This is the easiest way to begin to generate revenue.

In this chapter, I introduced you to the different ways that you can monetize your blog. Next, we're going to go even deeper and I'll share how much YOU can expect to earn from this career. Don't worry, in the coming chapters I will also walk you through how to set up a blog, get traffic, grow your subscriber list, and more. If you haven't already, go and check out my FREE blogging course at: http://www.salvadorbriggman.com/blogging.

# Chapter 2: How Much Money Can You Make Blogging?

I was at a networking event last week doing my thing.

I like meeting new peeps. It's hard to make new friends/connections in NYC, so I always try to get out and about.

100% of my customers find me online now, so I just go to these types of events to be social and have fun.

Yes, I'm a nerd.

Anyway, I was talking with this dude about my biz. He seemed cool. He was working on this new social networking startup.

All of a sudden, this older, but beautiful, brunette introduced herself and entered the conversation.

She was tall, lithe, and good looking. She visibly increased the tension in the room. Under any other setting, it would probably be hard to keep eye contact with her.

In the past, this is the kind of girl I would have TOTALLY gone after. Now, I'm happily dating someone. I started to share a bit of what I do, and how I started my own business, when she interrupted me...

**"I hear a lot of people say they're entrepreneurs when really, they're just unemployed."**

Ouch! Hahah.

Granted, the word "entrepreneur" is thrown around a lot now a days. It's kind of lost its meaning, wouldn't you agree?

I laughed, ignored the comment, and went on to explain how I'm a blogger, etc.

She gave me a weird look... ***"You can make money with that?"***

You'll find that this is a VERY common question.

Mainstream people can't really wrap their head around how you can work from home, make good money, and be your own boss.

I've been full-time as a blogger since 2014. It's nothing new to me. I still find it amusing that people find it socially acceptable to ask "how much do you make?" as a blogger.

In any other context, that question would be considered borderline rude. But, that's a small price to pay for being able to set your own hours, do work that you love, and live a life of tremendous freedom!

Now, you might wanna know how much money you can make so that you can figure out whether or not to spend time on this whole blogging thing. ***Right?***

Before we talk turkey, let me just say that making money from a blog is not something that you do over night. It takes time, consistent work, and a lot of learning.

For me, it took a year before I was able to go full-time on my first professional blog. In that year, I made ~$30k. The year after, I made $50k. It's been an upward climb since then!

**My Initial Sources of Income:**

- **Adsense:** This is Google's advertising program. You can put banner ads on your website and make money.
- **Consulting:** I was making money by offering consulting services.

- **Services**: I was offering a business service to my readers, which generated income.

This first year, I also wrote an ebook that I sold on my own website, but it didn't make a tremendous amount of money. It takes quality traffic to make good money from advertisements or affiliate marketing. It also takes knowledge and time to put together digital products.

Therefore, when you start out, your primary source of income is going to come from services or consulting. You'll be trading time for money.

### Can You Make Money Directly From Blogging?

Since a blog is free, the simple answer is no. The free content that you put out is meant to develop a relationship with a particular type of reader.

Once that reader is on your website, you can monetize their attention in a variety of ways. For the most part, this includes advertisements, sponsored content, digital products, services, and affiliate marketing.

### How Much Can You Actually Make?

The top bloggers don't really consider themselves to be bloggers. They're content marketers. As I've shared before, they use the blog to attract 'leads' and monetize those leads by selling them digital courses and products.

Now, of course there are fashion and entertainment bloggers out there that aren't selling these types of products. However, they're selling ***other people's*** products in the form of sponsorships advertising, and affiliate marketing,

At a certain point, a "professional blogger" might decide to use their excess funds to hire a team and turn their online presence into an education company or an entertainment company.

All of this being said, as an individual blogger, you can probably expect the upper tiers to make $100k – $200k max with **a lot of hard work** over a span of **5-10 years**.

This income is likely not solely derived from blogging. It probably also comes from services, products, affiliate marketing, etc. You can certainly make more than this, but at this stage, you're transitioning more into an internet marketer and using things like webinars to sell high ticket products.

A more **realistic goal** is to make between $30k – $80k, depending on how hard you're willing to work and the breakdown between selling services vs. other forms of monetization. Your niche also plays a big role.

Overall, the majority of bloggers don't make very much money at all. It's more of a hobby for them. If you want to make money, you gotta treat it like a business.

**What would YOUR life be like if...**

- You never had to report to a boss EVER AGAIN.
- You never had to commute to work in the rain, snow, and cold.
- You could work **whenever** you want, **wherever** you want (even if that's from a beach in Thailand).
- You could spend more time with your family, friends, and wife or girlfriend.
- You could FINALLY earn $30k, $50k, or $80k per year doing something that you love.

Imagine how it would feel to be able to wake up at a reasonable time, make a healthy breakfast, and check out a cool cafe in your area.

The cafe has a friendly staff and maybe one or two other professional types are working there with their laptops. They're banging away at their keyboard.

You order a drink and a snack and then sit down at a table close to the window. It's peaceful. Every once in a while, you can see some pedestrians walking past the cafe. You pull out your laptop and get to work.

You're there, sipping a steaming cup of coffee or tea, and working on a new blog article for next week. As you type on the keyboard, your mind is racing. You have so many ideas that are just flowing through your fingertips. You already know, this is gonna be a killer post!

How freakin' great would it feel to be able to say that was YOUR day?

Pretty epic, right?

Well now it can be...

**Let me introduce you to a career with:**

- **Job stability:** It will take some time to get set it all up, but once you do, you can't be fired. You are the boss!

- **Unlimited income potential:** You can make a much or as little as you'd like. Once you're earning $30k, $50k, or $80k per year, you can sit back and relax. Or, you can work to continue to earn even more money. It's up to you.

- **Passive income opportunities:** Visitors can stumble on your website without you having to be there. This allows you to earn money in your sleep. Your time won't be tied to your income.

- **Influence and authority:** In a small way, you can be famous! People will know who you are, without ever having met you in person. This makes you feel powerful and influential. Just don't let it go to your head.

- **Location-independence:** You can work from home, a cafe, or anywhere else. You don't have to report to an office location every day. You can spend your free time as you like.

All you gotta to do get started is **educate yourself!** And... you're doing that right now! Every worthwhile income-earning opportunity in life has required this.

If you want to become an accountant, you gotta go through 12 years of school and then 4-8 years of college and post-graduate work.

Not to mention that now a days the average cost of college is ***$34,000*** for private institutions and ***$9,970*** for in-state residents attending public colleges.

That isn't in total... that's PER YEAR.

This doesn't include other fees, special housing, or food.

Over four years, that's $136,000 that you'll be paying for the opportunity to earn a job that starts at ***MAYBE $30k – $50k.***

The funny thing is that if you want to earn more, you'll have to then pay for even more schooling, am I right? You can earn the SAME amount of income from the comfort of your home and it doesn't cost $136,000 to do it.

In this book, you will discover how to become a full-time blogger for a fraction of the cost.

**The Real Benefit of Blogging**

This can be summed up in one word... ***FREEDOM!***

Just imagine how awesome it would be to be your own boss. You don't have to commute to work every day. You can work from home, a cafe, a beach in a foreign country, or really, **anywhere** you want.

I've worked from a lot of different locations including:

- Co-working spaces in Manhattan
- Cafes in Brooklyn
- Other countries (Thailand, Cuba, etc)

Since you run your own life, you can also decide **when** you work. You don't have to wake up early if you don't want to.

Pretty cool, eh?

**So… is blogging dead?**

Not at all. The "heyday" of blogging was about 2005 – 2009. I started mine in late 2012. I **made $30k** when I went full-time about a year later. I think that most people see the popularity of online video and social media platforms and they assume that people don't read blogs any more.

This is 100% false. There are some factors that have changed in the blogging industry, most notably comments and SEO, but it's not going anywhere.

You can still start a blog today and be VERY successful. In the next chapter, I'm going to show you step-by-step how to start a professional blog quickly. I'll walk you through what you need to do to get started and be with you ever step of the way. Now that you have an idea of how much you can earn, it's finally time to get started!

# Chapter 3: How to Start a Blog

For me, setting up a blog was one big struggle. I hated figuring out all of the technical jargon. I didn't understand what to do (or how). It was ***so freakin' confusing*** that I almost gave up!

Well... I'm certainly glad I didn't give up. Otherwise, we wouldn't be here now. I wouldn't have had the chance to:

- Impact millions of readers with my blog
- Get cited by The New York Times, The Wall Street Journal, CNN, Forbes, and more.
- Meet really cool entrepreneurs and changemakers
- Earn a great income doing what I **love**

In the last several years, I've been blessed with a ton of success at an early age, and I owe it all to that very first decision to start a blog. Starting a blog will transform your business AND your life.

Before you know it, you'll have people around the world emailing you, following you on social media, and sharing your website with their friends. Hands down, blogging is the BEST form of organic marketing out there. I've gotten access to millions of website visitors for FREE.

The process for setting up a blog is more complex than it seems. You simply need to do three things: get a domain name and hosting provider, install Wordpress, start blogging!

Wordpress is the engine that powers the majority of online blogs. It's the backend dashboard that will allow you to upload images, publish blog posts, track visitors, and create the look and feel of your blog's website.

When you make changes on the backend of your Wordpress dashboard, it will display those changes to regular website viewers. This means that you can easily change the "theme" of your blog, the layout, and the various tabs on the homepage navigation. You can quickly publish posts and pages with the click of a button.

With this chapter, I'm going to show you how to easily set up a WordPress blog using the **best hosting provider** out there, Bluehost.

I use Bluehost to host my blog and many of my other websites online. Their service allows me to host a website with thousands of daily visitors, without breaking the bank.

For the special price of $2.95 per month, you'll gain access to:

- A FREE domain and website builder
- Powerful one-click WordPress install engine
- 24/7 support
- 30-day money-back guarantee!

This is a special offer that they're giving to fans of my first professional blog, CrowdCrux.

You can get started now with no risk and no hassle. This is the first step for setting up your blog. If you're not used to spending money on your business, $2.95 per month might seem annoying, but it's ***more than 50% OFF*** their usual price of $7.99 per month.

For that price, you're getting robust hosting, an easy-to-use WordPress install engine, unlimited support, AND a money-back guarantee.

Seriously, this is a steal.

(http://www.salvadorbriggman.com/bloghosting)

## Step #1. Register Your Domain Name

The first thing that you're going to need is a domain name for your blog. This is what people will "type in the address bar" to come across your website.

You can get your domain name right now and start the blog.

It took me a while to settle on the domain name for my blog. I created a list of ideas and eventually settled on "CrowdCrux" because all of the other ones were taken.

The first part of the name "crowd" was going to be the focus of this blog... crowdfunding. It's actually transformed into much more than that.

Now, I talk about building a crowd in general. How do you market your products, get your name out there, and grow a tribe of people who know, like, and trust you.

I chose the next part, "crux" because I wanted this website to be a hub of free educational content that people to use to get funding, grow their sales, and succeed in online business.

You can claim your domain name directly with Bluehost. (http://www.salvadorbriggman.com/bloghosting)

You'll just have to pick which package you'd like to go with. All of the packages (when you use my special link) will unlock a discount for you.

I'm using one of the more expensive tiers because I want access to SiteBackup. I also have multiple websites hosted on my account.

The more that you grow your blog and your business, the more you'll want to re-invest back into the company. It's the formula for long-term growth.

Once you select your tier, you can either:

- Claim a NEW domain name
- Assign your existing domain name
- Wait until later

Lastly, you'll just have to put in your standard information and finalize your order. You'll get the best possible pricing if you elect to choose the 36-month pricing package, at $2.95 per month or a total of $106.20.

This is one of the smartest decisions you can make. I've been with these guys for over 5 years and I wish I did this when I got started.

### Step #2. Buy Hosting For Your Blog

If you already have a domain name, or you didn't go through every step above, you're now going to have to buy hosting for your blog.

I know... hosting shouldn't cost money, right?

Like... everything should just be FREE, right. Ughhh!

The problem with a service being "free" is that there is NO customer service, TERRIBLE product quality, and POOR upkeep/updates.

Quality solutions cost a little bit of money, because they are **quality!**

How annoying would it be to have your website down all the time?

Wouldn't it suck to have **no help** setting up your site?

I don't know about you, but I hate outdated software. It's clunky, buggy, and doesn't work well. That's why I invest in robust hosting.

Let's be honest, the **$2.95 per month special price** for the 36 month package is NOT going to break the bank. You really only need the basic plan to get started.

(http://www.salvadorbriggman.com/bloghosting)

Usually, this hosting would cost a whopping $287.64 for the same timeframe. Today, you're getting more than 50% off that price, which comes in at $106.20.

Of course, if you wanted to, you could "figure it all out" yourself. You could download the WordPress open source code base, figure out how to upload it to a server, and deal with all the troubleshooting yourself.

That option comes with a price... your time (and sanity)!

This blog hosting provider has a one-click WordPress install feature, so you don't have to deal with any of that. It just works.

But, I don't take for granted the decision you have in front of you now. Should you start a blog, should you hold off?

What if it doesn't turn out the way you want? What if you're not able to earn income? What if people laugh at you online!

I had all of these same worries, apprehensions, and fears when I got started. I thought that people were going to leave angry comments and make fun of me.

I can say unequivocally that this will be the BEST decision of your life. Not only can you earn good income and get free traffic, but if you pour your heart and soul into your content, people will love it!

I very rarely get a troll, and usually, the claims they make are so outlandish that it's easy to just ignore them.

Blogging has allowed me to live a lifestyle where I can work from home (or anywhere), grow my revenue, drive traffic to new products, and instantly get credibility online.

Having one or two weird trolls a year is a small price to pay for the upside.

When you're ready to start the blog, here are the steps for buying hosting:

1. Go to Bluehost and click the green "get started now" button.
2. Pick the package you'd like to go with
3. Enter your desired FREE domain name (or assign one you already have)
4. Put in your contact or business info
5. Pay for your package
6. You're done!

**Step #3. Connect your domain name to your hosting account**

If you followed my steps in point #2, you don't have to pay attention to this section. You can skip it!

However, if you have a domain name with GoDaddy, 1&1, or some other registrar, you're going to have to assign this domain name to your Bluehost hosting account.

It's pretty easy to connect it. All you need to do is change your name servers (DNS) to:

- **ns1.bluehost.com**
- **ns2.bluehost.com**

The easiest way to do this is just to google "how to change name servers" for the domain registrar that you used. You could also google "how to connect Bluehost with…"

Once you change these name server entries on GoDaddy or 1&1, you just need to log into your Bluehost account, go to the addon domain tab, and add the domain to your account.

I know that this might seem overwhelming, but that's why we're using this hosting provider. They have 24/7 support!

Not only do they have a step-by-step outline of how to do this, but you can also call them up at any time and get guidance. You can even chat with them online.

These are the basic steps, summarized:

1. Assign your GoDaddy, 1&1, or other domain name to Bluehost by pointing your DNS nameservers to ns1.bluehost.com and ns2.bluehost.com.
2. Add your domain to the Bluehost hosting account by going to the addon domain section.
3. You're all good to go!

**Step #4. Install WordPress on Bluehost**

WordPress is the "backend dashboard" of your blog. It's responsible all of the functionality like:

- Publishing blog post
- Managing comments
- Generating visitor statistics
- Handling the "theme" or appearance of the blog
- Uploading images, videos, and more.

You're getting this all free! It works right out of the box. All you have to do is turn it on.

This literally takes seconds to install, thanks to the Bluehost one-click WordPress install feature. To get started, you'll just click the one-click install feature from your cpanel menu.

Then, you'll pick the domain name that you want to install this on. It's as easy as that! Make sure that you choose the correct domain name if you assigned multiple to your account.

While this is pretty simple, you can also get help and talk to a WordPress expert at any time. Just call the number and you'll get in contact with a member of their support team.

After you choose the primary domain name that you'll be using for your blog, you just gotta enter some basic info, like the site title, etc.

You can always change this information later. I've changed my password over the years for security reasons and I have also changed the website title.

Remember, write down your username, password, and email address that you enter on this screen. You'll be using this information later to log in to WordPress. You don't want to lose it.

And........ boom! You're done.

That wasn't so bad, was it?

Before I leave you, I want to give you a quick primer on how WordPress works, so that you can get started blogging right now.

All of the main functionality for the WordPress dashboard is found on the left side of the screen. The top bar sort of functions as "short cut" links for common actions, like creating a post.

Basic WordPress terminology and vocabulary:

- **Post:** This is the actual blog post text. When you create a post, you'll enter a title, message, and insert any media that you'd like. You can easily format it and see the changes in real time. Posts include categories, tags, and often times, a featured image.
- **Page:** The main difference between pages and post is that a post is a single piece of content, which resides in a certain "category" or in your post achieve. A page is a static page of your website, like your about page, and is usually found via your navigation menu.
- **Comments:** These are the responses that people write to you after reading your posts or pages. You can read through them, respond to them, and moderate them.
- **Media:** This is all of the images, video, and multimedia content that you use on your blog. You can insert this content into posts, pages, or link to it directly.
- **Plugins:** I was confused about these at first. Basically, plugins are little bits of code that you can install that will expand the functionality of your website beyond the standard WordPress functionality.
- **Appearance:** This is where the look and feel of your blog can be controlled. You can install free or premium WordPress themes to make your blog look more professional.
- **Widgets:** These will show up in the sidebar or other areas of your blog or website. You could put popular posts, archives, or subscription forms in your sidebar by the use of widgets.

When you're just getting started with WordPress, the first features that usually snag your attention are themes and plugins.

You can browse the free WordPress marketplace to look at all of the different themes that you have available to you.

At the same time, as we discussed before, free does come with a price. Usually, free themes are not very professional looking. They're kind of amateur.

This is one reason that I recommend investing in a premium theme to make your website look like it cost thousands of dollars to make.

In reality… you probably only spent $50 on a nice-looking premium theme.

A marketplace like Themeforest is an amazing source of high quality premium themes. You can download most of them for between $20 – $50. Epic!

I actually used Themeforest to get a website theme for my personal blog. It looks amazing.

I hope you've found this step-by-step tutorial to be helpful!

For me, starting a blog has been a career-shifting decision that has led to so many incredible opportunities.

If you want to get free traffic, grow a loyal following, and earn consistent income online, then you're making the right decision!

# Chapter 4: Write Killer Blog Posts

In school, you're groomed to talk, write, and think a certain way.

High school will have you write long essays with appropriately spaced paragraphs. You're told not to use "you" or "I" when you write, because it's not proper.

**What a load of B.S.**

Most of the writing rules that you were taught hold up if you're doing some kind of academic or corporate writing. However, if your goal is to persuade, entertain, educate, or touch the reader, then you're playing by the *wrong* set of rules.

You can already see how I'm breaking ALL of these rules. I've broken them time and time again on my professional blog, which has been visited by MILLIONS of website visitors.

Now, it's not like I've always been good at writing blog posts. In fact, I *sucked*. I was terrible. Looking back, I can't believe that people actually wanted to read my early work.

The only reason I've been able to turn blogging into a full-time career is... I stuck at it. I kept working on it. Slowly, I'd get better and better with each passing week.

After a year, I hit "expert" status and was able to rack up **THOUSANDS** and **THOUSANDS** of views for my work. I am now able to charge premium prices if I ever do freelance writing.

I want to show you how to do the exact same thing. By the end of this chapter, you'll have a crystal-clear path for writing better blog posts (and in less time).

If you read every word of this chapter and APPLY it, then you'll be able to:

- Charge higher freelancing rates
- Get more traffic to your blog posts
- Develop a cult following of readers that can't wait for your new content.

This is powerful stuff. In the wrong hands, it can actually manipulate consumers into buying things that they don't need. That's why I'm entrusting it to you. I believe that you will use this information ethically in order to share your authentic voice with the world. So, let's get into a few of the ways that you can write more effective blog posts.

**The Weird Way People "Read" Online**

People read online blog posts differently than books and magazines. They rapidly skim them, picking out the pieces of the article that are most relevant or most apparent.

It's almost like they have ADD.

Usually, someone will spend *so much time* looking for a helpful article online that they first must determine whether or not this is an article worth investing time reading. Then, once they've decided that the article will answer their questions, they start to skim it, starting with the headlines.

You can be sure that any bullet points, numbered lists, and pictures will easily capture their attention.

If I had to pick one word to describe how people read online it's "lazy." Readers are under the perception that they're busy and don't have a lot of time. Objectively, this is not true, but everyone will argue this.

They don't want to do any work to consume information online, so they'll resort to the easy-to-read parts of an article, like the titles or the first sentence of a paragraph.

My first articles online read like **_mighty essays_** with long paragraphs connecting the various ideas together. This was the **WRONG** way to write for an online audience. It assumes that people will be reading every word of your article.

Once you begin to write in a style and format that is easier to consume, you'll have much more success getting traffic to your blog.

**Your Headlines Are Your Article**

You can have the best written blog post in the world, but if it doesn't have an enticing headline and sub-headlines that both draw attention and summarize the article, then no one's going to read it.

I remember that the first time I heard this, I was furious. I was reading up on the subject of blogging from my dorm room in college. Up until that point in my life, I had been led to believe the substance matters more than anything else.

Not true!

Both in the online and the real world, appearance matters more than reality. The design of the book matters more than the contents. **Why?**

Because your initial goal is to get people to actually check out your work. In time, your goal will be to get them to actually read it and become a loyal subscriber. For now, we just need to get attention.

I used to think that if someone wrote a book with all of the secrets of the universe in it, then people would beat a path to their door. Instead, what would end up happening is **no one would read it,** because it's not hyped up enough.

There would be no marketing or sales behind the book to persuade people of the value of reading it. The secrets would be forgotten.

That's the sad truth.

I have personally put together educational content to show people EXACTLY how to achieve a particular result in their life. But, it is all wasted time, unless I spend an equal amount of time persuading people of their need to check out this content, consume it, and act on it.

Your headline and sub-headlines are what "sell" your article and convince someone to spend five minutes of their day reading it.

**You MUST Include Images In Your Post**

If you don't include images in your blog posts, you're missing out on valuable SEO juice and making it harder to understand your ideas.

First of all, relevant images will improve the overall SEO score of your post. Every bloggers should be striving to get to the top of google for their niche. Images help you to rank better in search engines.

Second, images will help someone quickly and easily get an idea of what your blog post is about, and when included throughout the article, they'll serve as markers that people can use to better understand what you're trying to say.

Naturally, the human brain is more likely to focus on images and video over text. This is the reason that social media networks like Facebook, Instagram, and Snapchat focus on images and video. It's more work to have to read a block of text, internalize it, and figure out how that information applies to your life. As they say, a picture is worth a thousand words.

If you fail to include images in your blog posts, you're missing out on a massive opportunity. Your posts will come off as amateurish. Even if you're a really good writer, it will be more difficult to maintain the attention of a reader.

**Use Bolding, Italics, Underlines, and Capitalization.**

In English class, you were taught to avoid injecting emotion into your writing. You were told to write with a dry business-speak style language.

This is great if you're trying to become a lawyer or you're going to send a company memo. It's not so great though for establishing a relationship with readers or getting them to feel something about you and your blog.

You can use bolding, italics, and capitalization to draw a reader's attention to what you're saying. Because something is bold, people are more likely to read it. They rationalize that it must be important.

When people see your capitalized words, it adds a heck of a lot more emphasis to what you're saying.

I'm talking to **YOU**.

(see how I did that).

It almost has the feel like I'm asserting something strongly, or even shouting it. The subtext is "wake up, this is important."

Assume that, for the most part, people are scanning your writing. If you want to really emphasize a part of your message, you can use these devices to make it stand out.

Basic psychology finds that when we see a bunch of things that are the same, and one is different, we'll notice the thing that stands out.

**Write in a Conversational Style**

The worst thing that you can do is keep the reader at a distance from you, the blogger. You would only do this if you were a journalist, and trying to be objective.

The only other reason you might do this unintentionally is if you are afraid about putting yourself out there. You're compensating by sounding robotic and adopting a personality that isn't your own. It helps you feel less exposed.

Instead, the goal should be to bridge the distance between you and the reader. You want the reader to feel like they know, like, and trust you. You want them to think you're transparent. They should have a sense of who you are.

When you write exactly like how you'd talk, you come off as a human being. You sound less stuck up. There are a few easy ways to adopt this type of writing style. First off, you should read all of your writing out loud. ***How does it sound?***

The way I'm writing **RIGHT NOW** is the same way I'd sound I was talking to you in person.

Make sense?

The other thing that you can do to adopt this kind of writing style is to use vernacular. That's just a fancy word for the "slang" we all use.

For example, you could say…

So… do you wanna learn how to write conversationally?

I'm gonna share with ya how to sound like you're ***literally*** talking to someone through the computer screen.

They'll read your words and be like, woah… that's Sal! He's a cool (good looking) dude who lives in Brooklyn, NY. **Hit me up ladies!**

Hahah, okay, maybe I got a bit carried away right there. But, the lesson stands out!

Use vernacular. Read your writing out loud. Don't try to sound like an "expert" by being pompous, formal, and strict with your language.

**Sell The Reader on Reading**

This is kind of a weird concept. It took me a while to fully understand it.

I'm a nerdy kinda guy. I love learning new things. I rarely need motivation to learn something knew. If I want to figure out how to get fit, I'll read tons of books, watch educational videos, go to the gym, etc.

You might be like this too!

The rest of the world functions a little differently.

The average person must be SOLD on doing something. They have to be persuaded and motivated why they should expend precious energy to do something, in this case, read your blog post.

It's not enough to just share good information with them. You also have to persuade them to read that information. This is where "selling the reader on reading" comes into play.

When someone stumbles on a blog post, they are usually looking to achieve something, solve a problem, or gain clarity on a concept.

We can even take THIS very chapter as an example. If you are reading this chapter, you're wondering how to "write better blog posts."

But, why would you want to write better blog posts? A good little technique is to add the words "so that" to the end of a desire.

"I want to write better blog posts, so that…"

How would *YOU* fill that sentence in?

You could want to write better, so that you can:

- Get more traffic to your blog
- Persuade people to buy your products
- Emotionally affect people and turn them into raving fans
- Grow your email subscriber list
- Make more money from your writing!

The more I know about your ultimate motivation, the better. Let's say that you want to earn more money from your writing. If I wanted to get you to read this blog post with a high degree of attention, I could say...

*"I used these VERY SAME writing techniques to compose better blog posts that would go on to generate THOUSANDS of dollars in sales for my business."*

In this example, I'd be using me as the person who got the result from the information I shared in the blog post. I could also use someone else...

*"I had one student, Alex \_\_\_\_, who I shared these techniques with six months ago.*

*Last week, he sent me an email saying he ended up making $4,730 in advertising revenue this month as a DIRECT RESULT of writing better blog posts.*

*His new posts got him tons of traffic, and now he doesn't even have to do any more freelancing work!"*

The handling of your article will get people's attention. Your initial text and text throughout the article should continue to "sell" why people should pay close attention to this blog post.

This is a surefire way to develop a close connection with your audience. Rather than skimming your work, they'll be treating it like their favorite novel. They'll be hooked on your every word.

I'd go so far as to say that the entire subject of writing can be boiled down into three core categories. Whether you're a struggling novelist or a millionaire marketer, you will fit into one (or multiple) of these categories.

Writing is good for three things:

1. Educating and informing
2. Persuading (think Sales)
3. Entertaining

I've thought about this a lot, and these are the ONLY categories that you can fit into with your writing career. You might be in multiple categories, but these are the three that comprise writing as a whole.

First, let's talk about educating and informing. This is what I'm really, really good at. But, you don't have to take my word for it. Just look at the MILLIONS of people online that have read my blog, CrowdCrux.

On this blog, I share tips, advice, and strategies that you can use to raise money with crowdfunding. I've written blog posts and books on the topic. In this context, writing can be used to explain "how to do something," whether it's start a business, make more money, build up muscle, or get a girlfriend.

People use your writing to better understand the RIGHT way to go about getting results in an area of their life. The writing is simply the medium used to share tips, information, mindsets, and strategies.

Under this category, you are physically writing words, but you're actually more of a teacher. The writing is just the teaching medium.

I've found that individuals that have a strong "nonfiction" or "education" writing skill set tend to do very well with blogging. It's easy for you to write helpful blog posts that get thousands of views online.

Your ability to educate readers through writing will end up getting you attention, potential students, and from a business perspective, generate a lot of "leads" which you can later turn into sales. Your skills in this area will make it easy to write blog posts, ebooks, physical books, and anything that is of educational value.

Educational writing is very different from copywriting. If you have a flair for educational writing AND you enjoy a bit of fiction writing, this is the perfect marriage of your skills.

These writers are usually the highest paid of the three, and for good reason. They turn words into dollars! Your well-written sales page or email can result in thousands and thousands of dollars in sales for a business!

The goal with this style of writing is to persuade readers to make a particular decision. That decision could be to attend an event, buy a product, or sign up for a service.

It's a mix of sales and marketing. It's a very specific type of writing called copywriting.

This category of writing includes elements of education, sales, and even some fiction writing. The ultimate goal is to make readers FEEL something when they read your "copy." You are trying to change their state of mind.

In fact, the best copywriters typically study fiction writers to see how they invoke curiosity and lead a reader through a story. These elements can be included in an email sequence that leads to a sale.

For example, let's say you're selling a product. You're telling a story about wrestling with some kind of problem.

Then, you could say *"I was about to give up... when I discovered something that would change my life forever and lead to a dramatic improvement in the results I was seeing.*

*Literally, this changed everything! No more fear, frustration, or confusion.*

*Without it, I'd still be worrying whether or not I can afford to buy groceries for my family.*

*Instead, I'm happy, healthy, and enthusiastic about coming to work every day.*

*I can rest assured, knowing that I'm able to provide for myself and my family from the comfort of my home. All I need is a computer and an internet connection!*

*Tomorrow, I'm going to share with you what I discovered. It's free and anyone can use it to see remarkable success with _____. No joke!"*

What I like about copywriting is that it combines different elements of writing AND it makes readers more likely to read every single word that I write.

We all have come across educational text. You probably didn't read it word from word. You skimmed it.

When you're drawn into a story, you'll read every word of it, waiting to find out what happens next. This is a very effective way to evoke emotions, curiosity, and capture attention.

Copywriting is a powerful way to enhance educational-style writing. You can use it to sell your books, products, and services. I think everyone into writing should learn it. It's not really talked about very much. I'm angry I wasn't ever introduced to it in school.

The final category can be summed up in one: entertainment. You could also use the word "artistic." I'd lump novelists, fiction writers, poets, and really anyone who is writing something that's meant to ***simply be enjoyed*** into this category.

Copywriters will use stories and emotionally evocative words to ***sell*** products. Novelists, entertainers, and artistic writers use these techniques to ***tell a story*** that makes someone think differently about the world.

It might take them feel something, or have a change of attitude about an experience in their life. Usually, after reading the book, they're not looking to purchase a product, a course, or become a student. If they liked the book, they'll just be waiting for the author to write their next book.

Unlike the other categories, which focus on getting the reader to take action, or become informed about their world, this category is designed to serve as a happy or interesting distraction from every-day-life.

You can read a story and get lost in it for a few hours. It might cause you to have thoughts about your real life, but at the end of the day, Harry Potter is meant to be enjoyed because it's an alternative realty.

Under this category, most of your energy and focus will not be on actual writing, though of course this is essential. You do need good descriptive, concrete, and punchy writing. However, there are many books that have great writing, but fail to sell copies.

Instead, your success will depend on your grasp of ***storytelling***.

Think of it this way... you can have a beautiful written book that fails to garner attention. On the flip side, you can have a book that has a 3rd grade reading level writing and it sells millions of copies.

Think Twilight, James Patterson, Nora Roberts, etc.

Storytelling skills are what make the difference between a bestseller and a book that sells less than 1,000 copies (which is most books).

No matter whether you're trying to educate, persuade, or entertain with your writing, I can help you build a blog that will replace your full-time job. This chapter covered some of the basics when it comes to writing killer blog posts that get views. However, I've gone way more in-depth in my blogging course. I'll link you to a free video course that leads into it. This free video will share a blogging secret. (http://www.salvadorbriggman.com/blogging)

# Chapter 5: How to Get A River of Traffic to Your Blog

One of the most frustrating things that I've EVER experienced is trying to get people to read my blog. It's maddening.

You spend hours and hours writing a killer article. You pour your heart and soul into the blog post. It's so rich with content and compelling writing, that you can't wait for the world to see it.

Finally, you publish it and... no one reads it. No one checks it out. No one comments.

All that work and no one can bother to read what you are sharing (for free) with the world.

Crazy, right?

In this chapter, I'm going to show you how to obliterate this problem. By using these proven techniques for getting traffic to your blog, you'll make it so that you instantly get an audience the second you hit "publish."

Just think how it would feel to **never have to worry** about this again.

If you follow these techniques, you'll get consistent, regular traffic to your blog articles, and everyone will wonder how you did it! I have used these same strategies to grow **multiple blogs** to thousands of views per month.

For example, I started my personal blog, SalvadorBriggman.com in 2014. On this blog, I share business advice and a slice of my personal life. You'll discover cool vlog videos, trips I've taken, and more. Here is a WordPress graph of the traffic to the blog. It shows how my traffic has grown from 2014 to 2015 to 2016.

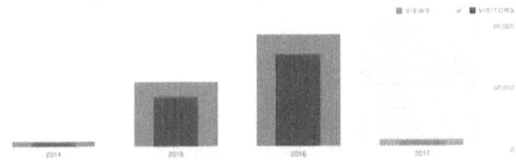

As you can see, this blog did a little over 50,000 views in 2016. Sweet, huh? Compared to 2015, this is a growth of 74.70%. That's a lot of new viewers discovering my work. Here's the kicker... I haven't paid for ads. By applying the strategies we'll discuss, you can get traffic to your blog just like this.

Now, let's take another example. I started another blog called PodcastingHacks.com in 2015 that shares tips and advice for starting a new podcast. I run a podcast myself, called Crowdfunding Demystified, which has been downloaded more than 150,000 times. Below, I'll share some of my visitor stats for the first few months since starting Podcasting Hacks and how it's performed from then on.

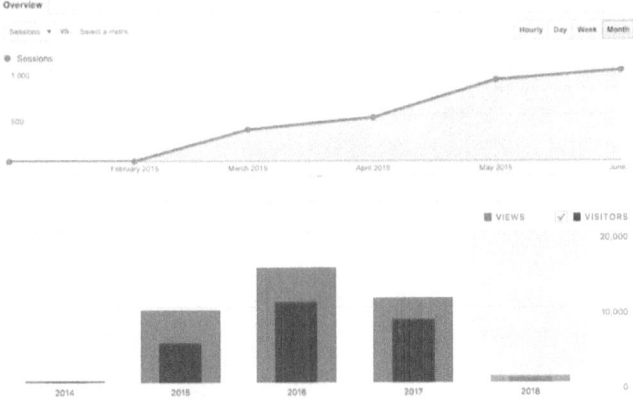

Within the first few months, I was able to grow this blog quickly to 1,000 users per month (and I was only blogging part-time). After that, I grew it to more than 10,000 views in the first year and 15,000 in 2016. That's a big increase and *I only published 5 articles in 2016.*

In 2017, my traffic went down a bit, but that's only because I literally *only published 4 articles* in the entire year. Seriously.

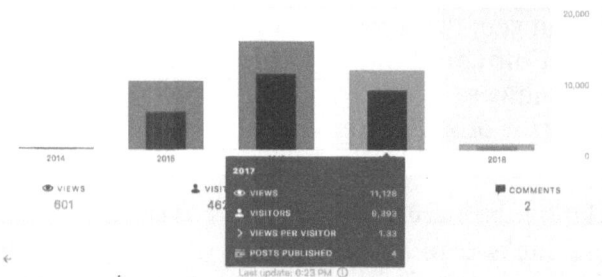

How is that I can command so much traffic with such little input? I barely wrote any articles in 2016 and 2017. Wouldn't be great to get 10,000 or 15,000 views to your blog and only have to publish 4 articles a year? Don't worry, I'll show you how in just a little bit.

Before I go through *exactly* what I'm doing to get this traffic, let me share with you one final example. My main blog, CrowdCrux.com, is my very first professional blog. I started this website in 2012 while I was a university student. It shares tips and advice about crowdfunding. I went full-time on this blog in 2014. Let's take a look at my stats from 2012 – 2015.

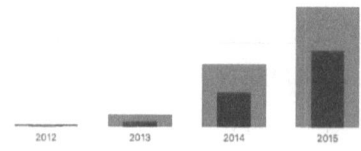

In 2012, my blog did 2,814 views. In 2013, it did 129,814. In 2014, it did 722,864. In 2015, it did ***1,418,835 views.*** Wow! That's the year that I broke the $50k income milestone and was cited by major media publications like CNN, The Wall Street Journal, The New York Times, and more.

To be honest, I actually have more blogs than this, but I don't share this to brag. I want to show you what's possible. As you can see, I've built up multiple blogs so that they're doing ***consistent traffic*** and require ***minimal maintenance.*** I just have to publish a post every once and a while.

Now, do you want to hear the great news? No matter what year it is, these strategies will **WORK** for you and your blog. They are tried and true methods of getting traffic and attention to your website. You just have to put them in place. They worked in 2012, 2016, and they ***continue to work*** today. Let's get started going through the different ways you can get traffic to your blog.

### Get Free Traffic With Social Media Marketing

Let's be honest, you know why social media is important and why you should care. Simply put, it's a traffic driver. It's a way to engage your customers and discover new ones. However, I feel like social media has become like the gym. Everyone knows why you should go, but no one actually goes.

There are three common excuses why new bloggers don't do social media.

**1. "I don't have the time."** This just means you have poor time management. There are software solutions like Buffer and Hootsuite to automate social media sharing. Personally, I love and use buffer.

**2. "Why would anyone care what I share?"** You won't be using social media to share thoughts like "My cat just rolled over."

You will be using social media as a tool to figure out what type of content your audience likes and what problems they experience.

Let's say you are in the business of selling men's clothing and a post that you shared titled "How to look good on the weekends" gets a lot of clicks and retweets. The problem: Your customers want advice on how to look good before going on a date. The solution: The article you shared promises a solution.

You may consider writing similar content on your company blog and then sharing it. In the long-term, it would attract readers to the blog, who are also part of your customer base. You will then have the opportunity to sell them on your products.

**3. "I'll do it later or once I have an audience."** Social media is like investing – the earlier you get in, the larger your returns and the easier it is to do, simply out of habit. You can use social media as a tool to either connect with an audience you already have or develop and attract a new audience.

To me, it's a no-brainer that if there is a *free* marketing platform out there, and you are not taking advantage of it for your business, you're missing out on a major opportunity. It's like you're using an old-school razor phone when everyone else has iPhones and can easily check their emails on the go. Maybe it doesn't matter in a personal sense, but in business, it will cost you money!

Even if you are willing to start building up your social profiles, many bloggers have difficulty getting started. You might not comprehend why on earth anyone would wanna follow you. At the end of the day, people will follow you for two reasons.

**1. You solve a problem they are experiencing.** The articles, tips, ideas, and advice that you share help them achieve their goals in some way. You should interpret this broadly. I follow some people simply to stay up to date on cutting-edge technology improvements in industries I care about.

**My problem:** I want to have the edge over all my competitors. I want to be able to put the pieces of the puzzle together faster than they can.

**My solution:** The news accounts and people I follow share the information that gives me that edge.

This type of content is ***logical***. People want to know how to get better at marketing and logically, based on your previous helpful shares, they will benefit from following you.

**2. You provide entertainment.** Ironically, this also solves a problem for people, but the distinct difference is that your content evokes an ***emotional response***.

Examples could include: quotes, stories, images, shocking or inspiring facts, etc.

This type of content is ***emotional***. People will follow you based on how they perceive you will make them ***feel*** in the future. You may make them feel inspired, motivated, or hungry to reach their goals.

The more that you share content, the more followers you will get. Every once and a while, you'll be able to share a link to your website, blog post, or a product that you've created. At that moment, you'll instantly realize the power of social media. Social media is a huge source of free traffic that you can use to grow your blog. I know ***I*** didn't believe that when I first got started, so let me prove it to you.

Below, you can see how much traffic social media has sent my blog!

| | | |
|---|---|---|
| 5. | twitter.com / social | **5,343** (0.78%) |
| 6. | facebook.com / referral | **3,524** (0.51%) |

All I did was take a few minutes to set up a Facebook and Twitter page. Then, I began to promote them more on the blog. I started putting out content more consistently. Over time, I amassed hundreds of thousands of followers across my various accounts. Pretty wild, right?

Of course, you must have the right social media strategy. You can't just ask people to check out your blog. You have to share articles or content that is genuinely improve the lives of other people. These articles should be entertaining, help readers solve problems, or clue them in to new events that they care about. Think of your blog as a mini media company.

I've found it the easiest way to begin to get some traffic to a new blog. Right now, take a second to create a social media account for your blog on the major networks like:

- Facebook
- Twitter
- LinkedIn
- Instagram

You'll thank me later. Once you do have all of these different social media accounts, you'll start to get traffic, but you'll also begin to think, "wow – this is taking up a lot of my time." It's true. It takes time and energy to create posts and have them go out on your social media profiles.

I don't mind working hard, but I am a big believer in working SMART. What does it mean to work smart? I define it as spending no more time on a task than is required. I don't want to spend my valuable time doing something if I can outsource it, assign it to an employee, or find a software tool that will do the same thing.

In the early days, I had a BIG EGO and I thought that by doing EVERYTHING, I was showing people that I was a "boss" at life. I could handle anything, work long hours, and get the job done.

This isn't "cool." It's just stupidity. But, I was young, haha!

Not only was it inefficient, but it also led to me getting burned out. I was spending all my time on menial tasks and ignoring the bigger issues I had to deal with.

Around this time, I started to automate the majority of my social media. I'm not talking about replies, just posting. I developed a posting schedule and pre-scheduled content weeks in advance to go out on my accounts.

This saved me time, headache, and made it so that I only had to spend 30 minutes on social media every month.

To do this, you're going to need to sign up with a social media management software solution, like Buffer, Hootsuite, or Edgar. This software tool will take all of the frustration and time out of having to schedule posts to go out on your social media accounts. It's a godsend!

If you do nothing else, do this. I promise you, this is going to save you SO MUCH time going forward. You'll thank me later. The more content that you pump out on a consistent basis, the larger your following will grow.

Once you've gotten your social media profiles up and running, you're in business! You'll start to see a trickle of traffic flowing to your website, which we'll later build into a raging river of visitors and raving fans. The next step in the process is to create a guest posting strategy.

**Build Your Traffic With Guest Posting**

There's a great way that you can kill two birds with one stone. Not only can you use this to get ***more traffic*** to your blog, but you can also gain ***valuable*** backlinks, which improves the domain authority of your website (we'll get into that more in the next section).

Yes, I'm talking about "guest posting." This simply refers to writing blog posts for other blogs in exchange for a back link to your own.

I've seen this strategy used extremely effectively by many of my female friends who write in the fashion, design, and personal development niches. It's also worked for other bloggers that follow my work in the business and marketing categories.

All that you have to do is approach a blogger who has an audience that is similar to yours. Shoot them an email and offer to write a completely original article for their blog. You can brainstorm some topic ideas that will be relevant to their audience. In exchange for this free article, the only thing that you want in return is a link back to ***your blog*** somewhere in the article and to be credited as the author. No biggie.

This does two things. One, it gives people an easy way to discover your website. If people like the content, they are going to see what else you have to offer. This means you're going to see an influx of traffic from the article. Second, it bumps up the authority of your blog, because you're getting a backlink from a reputable source. I'll talk more about SEO in the next section.

When it comes to guest posting, most bloggers will do this once or twice over the course of 6 months, which is great. However, I'm advocating something much more intense. I'm talking about contributing a guest blog post every single month (if not more). By doing this, you're ensured to see a huge jump in your traffic and subscribers. This is a proven strategy to grow your influence online. Many other bloggers have used it to get started. Go hard on it!

You can also reach out to other influencers via Instagram, YouTube, or those that host podcast shows and pitch them on your expertise. You can show them that you have valuable tips that you'd be happy to share with their audience. If they say yes, you'll instantly gain access to an entirely new community, which will send more traffic to your blog.

I recently had one guest on my podcast who delivered great value for the audience. He also pitched his services and how he could help my audience with problems related to their business. From coming on my show, they ended up making $26,000 in agency revenue as a result! This underscores the power of "tapping in" to someone else's audience.

## Get Free Organic Traffic (From Google) With SEO Optimization

I hate that term "SEO Optimization." Every time I hear it, I think "yada yada yada." My eyes just kind of glaze over. I know that it might sound boring, but I want to share with you the real value of SEO Optimization and why it's such a crucial pillar of a thriving blog.

Free traffic from Google is elusive for most. They'll follow everything that these SEO experts tell them, but they don't see much in the way of real results.

The only reason that I started to see ***results*** from search engine optimization is because I read an entire book on SEO. This book went through the various ranking signals that Google uses to determine whether or not they should include your website in search results.

It was very enlightening. About 3 months after I started applying these new strategies, I began to see a ***massive surge*** in the amount of traffic that I was getting from Google.

Now, the vast majority of my traffic comes from search engines like Google. This is repeat traffic that I get day after day, month after month. In my opinion, SEO traffic is the holy grail of blogging. It's the reason that full time bloggers only have to work one or two hours per day to maintain their income streams.

If there's one word that you want to take away from this section, it's the word "domain authority." Your domain authority determines how highly you will rank in search results when someone types something in to the Google search engine. If you have a high domain authority, you will out rank other websites for that key term.

This is your virtual "report card" that Google assigns your website. Naturally, websites like the Wall Street Journal or Forbes have a high domain authority. Your new blog has a very low domain authority. The more that you can improve this number, the better.

As a blogger, you gotta begin to consciously work on the domain authority of your website. Before we get into a few ways to do that, let's take a quick look at some of the major ranking signals that Google takes into account when determining the "domain authority" of a website. Three major ones include:

1. **Backlinks and link score:** The quality and quantity of the back-links to your website. When other blogs or websites link to yours, it increases your domain authority. You are more likely to rank higher for certain key terms.

2. **Content:** Google can only "crawl" and understand your content to a certain extent. Things like keyword usage, length, comprehensiveness, and titles will impact the quality of the content.

3. **Technical Setup:** The page speed, security, and mobile-friendliness of your blog will impact your SEO score.

It's Google's job deliver relevant information to users on they're searching for. They will judge your content based on the above factors when trying to figure out how well your content fits their search query.

Over time, relevant and authoritative inbound links to your blog's domain name and its individual pages are weighed very heavily. For example, you might run a fashion blog and get recommended and linked to by a fashion blogger. This is a great link that will boost your website's SEO profile.

One of the issues with many websites is that they over do the search engine "optimization" part, by using unnatural anchor text, getting links from spammy websites, having duplicate content, and being too aggressive with their on-page optimization. This can have a negative effect on your SEO and get you flagged as a spammer in the eyes of Google.

Take a second and put yourself in the shoes of a prospective blog reader and answer these questions:

- What problems do they have and what would they type into Google?
- How would they describe the problem when they search for it?
- What words would a prospect type into YouTube, Amazon, Google images?

These questions are the first layer when considering how to craft your blog article. If you use the right keywords, you will have a better chance of ranking in Google for those terms. Below, I'll include a few simple ways to improve the SEO of your blog.

- Include keywords in the titles of your articles
- Make sure the permalink of your post is optimized
- Actively work to get backlinks from other websites.
- Write both list-style articles and comprehensive 2,000+ posts

- Link to websites that are similar to your blog's subject. It gives more indications to Google regarding what your website is about.

- Use headlines like H2 to help search engines understand your content.

Google really likes niche websites that are authoritative about a particular topic. The key to boosting the traffic to your blog is to stay consistent. Produce content regularly around a specific topic. Over time, you'll become an authority on that topic in the eyes of google. The more that other websites link to you, the higher your domain authority will become.

**Share Your Articles in Social Media Groups**

Another way that you can get traffic to new blog articles is to share them in social media groups on Facebook, LinkedIn, Google+, and on online forums. I don't recommend spamming social media groups, but if you share articles that will be beneficial for the group, you'll usually be okay. For example, I recently shared an article that I wrote on Google+. In the article, I talked about how some of the most popular podcasters are manipulating the iTunes algorithm.

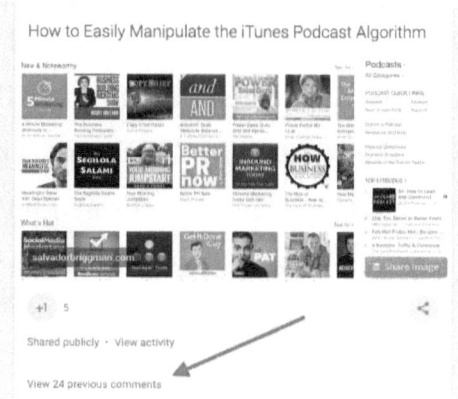

This post lead to over 24 comments, discussion, traffic, and new subscribers. When you share your article, you ALWAYS have to be 100% okay with any controversy or discussions that come about. You're putting your work out there for the world.

For one of my blogs, I have a few LinkedIn groups that I post in on a regular basis. The moderators know me and know that I produce high quality content. Last year, according to google analytics, this has sent my other blog 600+ views.

| linkedin.com / referral | 693 | (0.10%) | 49.21% |

And that traffic is all free!!

The great thing about sharing your articles in social media groups is that you'll quickly see what readers think of your work. This will help you fine-tune your writing and craft better blog posts in the future. In my experience, readers are more likely to leave comments in social media groups than on your actual blog article. It's just easier for them.

Sharing your work can be intimidating at first, which is why I invite you to get started in my new Facebook group, which is all about blogging! You can share your blog, new posts that you're writing, or ask any questions that you have about blogging. This is an easy way to get started putting yourself out there.

(https://www.facebook.com/groups/325505794532370/)

**Turn Your Email List into Instant Traffic**

Logically, you probably know that if you were to focus on building an email list, you could use that list to get traffic to your blog posts, right? You can intellectually ***know something***, but at the same time, ***fail to take action*** on that knowledge. That is very, very common when it comes to business and life.

I can't tell you the number of bloggers that I've spoken with who have built up an email list from their blog, but fail to use it! They don't announce new articles to that email list for *fear* of "backlash" or that people might unsubscribe.

You should be sending out emails to your email list once per week. You can deliver them consistent value with new articles or resources. Over time, as you build up your email list, you'll cultivate a close relationship with your readers, which will make them more likely to invest in your products and services.

Over time, your email list will become a dependable source of INSTANT traffic that you control.

It's pretty powerful! Professional bloggers will build up an email list that they can use to:

- Announce new articles
- Unveil new products
- Direct readers to a particular website

Building an email list of blog subscribers is a very important topic that I want to devote more time and attention to. That's why this next chapter is all about how to actually build up that list of subscribers.

In this chapter, you've discovered a few different ways to get traffic to your blog. As you've seen, it goes beyond simple social sharing or "hoping" someone will discover and reference your work. I reveal even more methods in my blogging course, along with a secret about blogging (which you can find out here: http://www.salvadorbriggman.com/blogging).

Next, I'm going to share with you how to build up your list of blog subscribers and raving fans. These are the people that regularly read your work, share your articles, and buy your products. No joke, when used correctly, the information in the next chapter has the power to turn you into an internet celebrity.

# Chapter 6: How to Attract Raving Fans and Loyal Readers

Do you want more followers?

Do you want to build a large email list of subscribers?

With a large following, you can do almost anything online. You can launch a new business, write a book, or even host live events. A following gives you **POWER**. It serves as a real asset. It allows you to access people that you normally wouldn't be able to.

In this chapter, I want to show you how to get more people to follow *your* blog. It's not as difficult as you think. You just have to use strategies that work!

I've spent a lot of time building up a blog to more than 20,000 email subscribers. I know what works and what doesn't. You can use the knowledge I've accumulated to supercharge your blog and become a full-time blogger FASTER.

**Why followers will supercharge your blog...**

You never want to compete on price. It's the dumbest thing that you can do. Unless you're Amazon or Walmart, you're going to lose.

Instead, you want to compete on value. You want to bring more value to your customers than your competitors.

The great thing about having followers is that they are already "bought in" to you, your brand, and the solutions you're offering the world. This makes it very easy to transition them into customers of your business. You can also use these followers to convince more followers to join your cause.

Having followers will supercharge your online business because it makes you, your brand, and your business more valuable. You can drive traffic to products, links, and other resources. This will make other entrepreneurs want to be your friend and network with you.

I can't tell you the amount of good business deals I've gotten just because I have a following online. You get preferential treatment.

**How long will this take?**

One of the most common questions that I get is... how long will it actually take to build up a following of raving fans?

The real answer is that it depends. Some people have done it within a few months. Others have taken years.

I think a good answer is that if you're blogging consistently, sharing your posts, and following all of the strategies that I share in my blogging course, then you should see results in the first 3 to 6 months.

The hardest part of the journey is the beginning. You're going to be working really hard until you get to your first 1,000 subscribers. After that initial buildup period, things get much easier. You'll start making more money and you'll have a little community that will share your articles online, which will rope in more readers.

One of the laws in life is that the rich get richer and the poor get poor. I hate to say it, but it's true.

When you're already making $100,000 per year, it's easier for you to make an extra $5k. If you're only making $20k a year, then $5k is harder to come by.

The same goes for an online following. When you already have 10,000 followers, it's easy to use those network effects to rope in even more followers.

It's just one of those laws of the universe.

**How can you speed up the process?**

There are only two ways to speed up the amount of time that something takes.

1. Work harder (and spend more time working).

2. Spend money to speed it up.

If you're a young entrepreneur, then you have a lot of time. You can spend months or years of your life figuring out how blogging works. Then, you can apply those strategies and principles to grow your blog.

If you're in your late 20s, 30s, or beyond, then you don't have as much time. You'll want to adopt the mindset of spending money to *speed up time.*

For example, with my online blogging course, I share with you my best strategies, techniques, and tips for rapidly growing a blog. This program costs money, but it will accelerate your progress. You'll find that you quickly make back this initial investment, and then can on to invest in yourself in other ways.

**How to Get More Email Subscribers**

Your email subscribers are your blog subscribers. These are the loyal readers that will comment on your articles, share your posts, and follow your work. They form the foundation of your fan base and are a vital part of monetizing your blog.

Often times, when I'm coaching new blogging students, they will play favorites to the ways and methods that they *like* to go about collecting email addresses. They might prefer a subtle "ask" at the end of an article, rather than an in-your-face popup.

Unfortunately, this isn't the recipe for blogging success. You can't allow your emotions to play into business decisions. When you favor one method over another, you're allowing the ***artist*** inside of you to dictate how the ***business*** should be run. You won't get very far if the artist side of you runs the business.

For example, one time I was coaching a student and asked them why they didn't include a simple pop-up opt-in on their blog (which I'll get into next). They said, ***"I just don't like how it looks."*** I went on to ask them whether or not it got results. Did that popup lead to new email subscribers? They said, ***"Yeah, I guess it did. I should probably put that back on, but I just haven't had the time"***

If you want to become a full-time blogger and owner business owner, you don't have the luxury of half-heartedly trying out things or catering to your emotional whims. You have to apply effective strategies that work to get results. This is how professionals approach blogging.

### Step 1: Set up Opt-In Boxes

You want to make it as easy as possible for readers to join your blog's email list. There should be multiple places where they can enter their name and email address. Otherwise, website visitors will miss out on the opportunity.

We're all very busy and, as you know from previous chapters, we tend to skim whatever we're reading online. This leads us to ignore or simply not notice many opt-in boxes on website. In other words, we've been trained to ignore advertisements!

To get more email subscribers, you're going to want to set up a few different opt-in boxes throughout your website including places like:

- Your blog sidebar
- Your navigation links
- An "alert" bar that scrolls down the page (ex: HelloBar)
- End of the blog post opt-in form.
- Opt-in opportunities throughout the blog post

Having multiple places where a visitor can subscribe will increase the likelihood that they actually do. You never know where a reader's attention might be draw. Also, if your content is good, they won't mind these different opt-in boxes. There are many tools out there online to help you set up opt-in boxes like Optin Monster and Sumo.

**Step 2: Set Up Pop-Up Opt-ins**

A pop-up opt-in is a simple box that will appear as a popup on your website when a visitor starts to read an article. You've probably seen these around the web. They ask you to enter your email address to gain access to a free report or to join the website's newsletter.

You can use a simple plugin like Optin Monster to add this functionality to your blog. You might think that popups will annoy your visitors, but actually, I saw a MASSIVE increase in email subscribers when I installed Optin Monster.

Before I installed the plugin, people were coming to my website and I'd see a trickle of email subscribers. I thought that I was doing well. However, after I installed it, I started to see a regular stream of subscribers. All of a sudden, I realized that for many months, I had been missing out on all of those potential subscribers. Oops!

You see, initially, while I was getting traffic to my website, it wasn't converting as well as it could have. The popup helped to capture some of these visitors who just weren't aware of my existing subscription links. In general, popups serve to:

- Capture attention
- Present an offer to your visitor
- Track opt-in rates and split test your offers.

When you split test your offer, you can easily see how one offer converts better than another because your opt-in rate goes up. It's a data-driven approach to getting more email subscribers.

**Step 3: Create a Lead Magnet**

There are many different ways that you can grow an email list to thousands of subscribers. One of the best ways that I've seen is to begin to direct traffic to a specific landing page (more on that in a second) with some type of lead magnet.

That lead magnet could be a free ebook, checklist, guide, or other helpful resource. This is something that a visitor will gain access to when they enter their email address. You can think of it as a bribe. Other lead magnets could include:

- White papers
- Exclusive videos
- Free courses
- Access to a forum or Facebook Group

A visitor is more likely to enter their email because they'll be getting something tangible out of it. They'll get some free value. Make sense? Take a few minutes and brainstorm on a piece of paper a few different lead magnets that you could offer YOUR audience.

**Step 4: Build Landing Pages**

The second thing that I did that had a powerful effect on the growth of my email subscribers was to begin to use a landing page software tool like Leadpages. You don't have to use Leadpages, but it's what I use. The reason that landing pages will boost your subscriber count is threefold:

1. **You'll be able to optimize for a conversion.** There is only one thing someone can do who comes to the landing page, subscribe to your email list. You can see how wording and image changes affect this goal.

2. **You'll gain access to simple, but professional-looking design tools.** We tend to judge the quality of businesses online based on their design. If you have crappy design, people assume you're an amateur.

3. **You can present an "offer" more effectively.** This offer could be an ebook, a webinar training session, a free online course, a checklist, and more. You can list out the benefits of the offer and use other tools like count-down timers to persuade visitors to subscribe.

Below, you can see a very simple example of a webinar registration page that I created. It's not super fancy, but there is only one thing that my visitors can do... sign up for the webinar.

CrowdCrux

Keep in mind that visitors that I send to this page already know what I look like, because of my YouTube videos. They also know that I'm an expert in my space, so they don't need much convincing. The count-down timer helped to create a sense of urgency.

Looks pretty dumb and boring, right?

Don't hate! (haha)

Let's take a look at the results. Numbers speak for themselves.

This simple webinar had a sign-up conversion rate of about 75%! Can you IMAGINE how big your email list would be if 75%

of the people who came to your website signed up for your email list?

I made a decent amount from this webinar too. Your ultimate goal should be to monetize your email list, not just inform them of your new content.

Leadpages gives you all of the tools that you need to set up a landing page fast. I use them myself for webinars, giveaways, and to convert website visitors into email subscribers.

Having an email list will help you increase your traffic to new blog articles. You'll instantly get readers commenting on new articles and sharing them on social media networks.

This is the reason that for the first few hours, even when a big internet celebrity like Tim Ferriss publish a blog post, there won't be any comments. He and others won't start to get comments and social shares until he sends it out to his email newsletter.

**Step 5: Turn Subscribers into Raving Fans**

Every single person on your email list is a human being. They have thoughts, feelings, families, friends, credit cards, bank accounts, hopes, and dreams. Let me ask you this, if you were going to ask a favor of someone, would you rather have access to:

- 100 friends
- 500 strangers

Almost everyone would pick friends. Why? Because these are people that already know, like, and trust you. There is shared history. They have a sense of who you are. They care about you. I ask you this to illustrate the point that numbers don't matter.

You can have 10,000 people on an email list, but if they are just random strangers, then that big number is useless. I would rather have a responsive email list of 1,000 people who know, like, and trust me rather than a list of 10,000 random people.

It's not enough to just collect email subscribers with the methods that we covered above. You also have to warm these people up to who you are and the value that you can add to their life. The more that they:

- Read your articles
- See your name or face
- Hear your stories

The more they will come to trust you and believe that you are credible to talk about your topic. This is a simple process that can take a few days, a few weeks, or a few months. It really depends on how good your emails are.

An easy way that you can speed up this process is to make these subscribers FEEL something towards you and your work. You want to trigger emotions and get them to open up to you. There are many ways to go about this, but one effective strategy is to build anticipation.

Think of a new blog post as a "mini-launch." Your readers should be eagerly awaiting your next article, thinking about all of the amazing insights, tips, or benefits that it will bring to their life. When you release it, you'll see a spike in traffic because of the anticipation that you built up in your following. I'm going to outline a few different ways to accomplish this enormous task.

### Curiosity Leads to Anticipation

Let's take a look at the dictionary definition of the word anticipation. Anticipation is the "the act of looking forward" to something or "pleasurable expectation."

Before you begin to look forward to something, you first need your curiosity aroused as to what's about to happen. It's the same feeling that you might get waiting in line for the opening of an Apple store, wondering "what a new product is gonna be like."

To get someone into that mental state of "anticipation" you first have to gain their attention by evoking curiosity. Curiosity is a code word for "interest" or "attention." You gotta let them know that something is coming (and why they should care).

If you picture your reader sitting at home, they might be thinking "Hmm... I wonder what Bob is going to announce next week?"

These are a few easy ways to do this including:

- Hinting at what an article reveals, without giving away all the information.
- Secretive tips, stories, or revelations
- Saying how they'll feel, but not why they'll feel that way Ex. "you'll be so surprised!"
- Highlighting what they'll get out of the post
- Showing parts of the finished article to tease it

Rather than unveiling your blog post all at once, you're giving someone a glimpse of what it could be. By withholding some of the information, it evokes curiosity!

**Make Attractive Promises**

The next way to build anticipation leading up to a blog post unveiling is to make attractive promises. These should be promises that make your customers' ears perk up. When someone hears what you promise that your insights can do (or do for them), they should think, "No way.... really?"

You'll find that a lot of Buzzfeed headlines do this. A lot of news stations also do this before they go into a commercial. They'll say things like "And after the commercial break, you'll see why so many kids are getting addicted to this new game (and how to keep yours off it)."

This promise that "you'll see why after the break" is what builds anticipation to hear the story and is what maintains your interest throughout the commercial so that you don't go and watch another channel.

Your new article should DO something for the reader. It should either do something directly for your readers, like give them tips, or it changes their perspective in some way. If you make attractive and bold promises leading up to the announcement, then you'll get people to "tune in" when the blog post is published.

**Build Social Buzz**

Another extremely effective way to make people anticipate your launch is to build social buzz. No, I'm not talking about social media. I'm talking about underscoring what OTHER PEOPLE are saying about your work, or how they're behaving with regards to this upcoming announcement.

Let's say that you're trying to get more attention for your blog. You don't have many posts up, but when you do show people an article, they love it! They're saying things like, "Oh my gosh, that's a really good insight." or "No way! I totally get it now!"

You can use these early testimonials to build even more buzz for your blog. I don't know about you, but if a ton of people are loving a movie that's playing in theaters, then I'm definitely more likely to see it.

We use other people to help with our decision making. If other people are loving a blog post, we're going to spend some time looking into it. If other people are excited, we get excited.

**Real Blogging Success Story...**

With this chapter, you've discovered several effective ways of growing your list of blog subscribers. You can easily implement these and start to reap the rewards. In the next chapter, I'm going to share a REAL blogging success story. This is an ordinary person, just like you, who isn't a marketing expert or some kind of technology guru.

I took them under my wing and shared exactly what they needed to do to begin to get traffic and subscribers for their blog. They implemented my advice and within a few months, they saw a ton of new people discovering their work online. This led to new freelancing gigs, a jump in email signups, and even big media publications took notice.

# Chapter 7: A Blogging Success Story...

After I started to see success with blogging, I had several friends take notice. They asked me questions like, *"How can you make money with that?"* and *"How many hours do you work?"* I happily answered their questions, as I have answered yours. In previous chapters, I revealed how bloggers earn income, get traffic, and develop a loyal following. I'll also show you later why blogging is such a rich source of passive income.

Of all of these friends who took interest, one stood out to me, Shelcy Joseph. It's rare that I meet a young student who is focused, ambitious, and willing to work. She was all of these and more. Having immigrated from Haiti with her two sisters, Shelcy has been the quintessential New York City hustler that will work as hard as it takes to be successful.

The funny thing is, looking at her in person, you'd never think it. With an alluring sense of fashion, a model-like lithe body, and sun-touched skin, Shelcy has attracted a massive Instagram following with more than 7,000 devote fashionistas. After appearing in one of my vlog videos on YouTube, my followers were taken back saying, *"Shelcy is so beautiful and her accent is lyrical!"*

The moment that I met her, I knew that this new student had great potential. Shelcy was a powerful writer, a compelling storyteller, and had an eye for esthetics and fashion. Having already gotten great feedback on LinkedIn and Medium, I knew that blogging could unlock much of her talents. Together, we got to work starting her blogging career.

At first, everything went smoothly. Shelcy took all of my teachings to heart and she regularly attended classes and events related to online marketing, blogging, and social media. She was a quick study and started to pick up the basics of how to market herself.

Only, there was one **big problem.** After several months, she still hadn't launched an actual blog. She had come up with every excuse in the book and always put off launching a new website when I brought up the topic. I was very proud of all the learning she was doing, but it was finally time to take action. To put it simply, she wasn't following through.

Let me ask, does this sound like you? It certainly has been **ME** in the past. At different times in our lives, we all will put off taking action. We'll get caught in a cycle of "learning more" about a subject, when really, it's just a diversion from fear. We end up procrastinating through learning. At a certain point in time, the classroom lectures gotta stop and you need to get into the field. You **MUST** take action.

I knew that Shelcy was scared. I was scared also before I launched *my* blog. Actually, it was a mix of emotions. I was feeling excitement, fear, anxiety, and worry (about what my friends would think). The funny thing about emotions is that sometimes, no amount of talking or reasoning can change them. I came to the realization that I need to adopt a firm "coach" mentality. The kind of football coach you might not like hearing from, but who's candor and passion you appreciate once you've won the Super Bowl.

The next time I had a coaching session with her, I was very direct, and quite frankly, a little rude. I told her that based on her current progress, I didn't see her launching her website for another year or longer. I think I said something to the effect of, **"You're never really going to launch this thing."**

Oh boy, did she get angry. Very angry. She called me insensitive. She was annoyed and didn't like how I talked to her. Deep down, I think that she felt attacked. I had hit a nerve, and she didn't like it. To be honest, she was very close to just storming out of the coaching session all together. But, something different happened.

After we both calmed down, Shelcy decided to take what I had said as a CHALLENGE. She was determined to prove me wrong. Over the next few days and nights, she worked super hard to get everything together for the launch of her new blog. This included writing the first few articles, coming up with the name, setting up the hosting, and putting together a marketing plan.

I watched from the sidelines, secretly hoping that my "tough stance" would pan out. I didn't want to shy this student away from blogging, but it was now or never. Sometimes, you need that extra push to get started.

The day that I got a text saying her "blog was live" was a very happy day for me as a teacher. I knew that her entire life was about to change. I can be a tough teacher, but I'll get you results.

You see, until you actually launch your blog, it's just an idea in your head. People can't read your thoughts or experience your feelings. They don't know that you're an expert on a particular topic.

A few months after launching this blog, Shelcy started to get freelancing clients, writing gigs, and emails from her fans. You can read one of the texts that a fan sent her below. Paraphrased, it reads, *"Hi, I have been reading some of your posts and I am interested in the career development coaching you offer. I am struggling to figure out the direction I want to go in, how to position myself for the growth I want, and the best way to showcase the diversity in my skill set without putting myself in a box."*

This fan initially started to follower her on LinkedIn, but once she had a website, was able to read her other articles and contact her via email. A website gives you legitimacy. Even if you've been publishing on other platforms like LinkedIn, it's the best way for clients and readers to interact with you. It can get you consulting clients, freelancing work, product sales, connect you with advertisers, and more.

Your website is the hub of all of your activity. You'll use it as the home base for all of your social media traffic and promotion. I can't emphasize enough how important it is to have your own domain name.

The blog that Shelcy founded is called A Millenial's Guide to Life. It's a career-focused blog dedicated to the multi-passionate millennials (aka multipotentialites) who want to make a living by doing all the things they love. In addition to this blog, Shelcy has an Instagram account called NYCxClothes, which features New York Stories, fashion, and her lifestyle.

In the last few years, she's been cited by Forbes, The Penny Hoarder, Neil Patel, and more. She's grown a small events and freelancing business in New York City. A number of her achievements have astounded me, including how she now earns more than $1,500 per month from Instagram.

Along with setting up a profitable freelancing business, Shelcy also runs events in New York City to bring together young professionals. Some of these classes include: Mindful Meditation, Paint & Sip Fun, Essential Oils & Body Scrub Workshops, Creative Work Sessions, and more. The events demonstrate how as an influencer, you can have your "fingers in multiple pies" or be able to monetize many of your different passions.

You can learn more about Shelcy and her incredible blogging journey when you sign up for my FREE blogging course that accompanies this book. You'll directly from her and discover exactly how her life has changed as a result of her blogging career.

In the remarkably candid interview, Shelcy opens up and shares her entire story with you. She reveals how she:

- Earns money
- Gets traffic
- Tips that she has for other bloggers

Blogging and online business is different from a traditional career path. You're not going to find a quality class in college on "blogging." If you want to succeed, you need to learn from people who are where you want to be. You have to be willing to learn from their success.

You might not care about the "business" side of blogging, but it's what enables you to make a living from it. Shelcy says, *"I realized the one thing I really care about: storytelling. In fact, writing was always the activity that made me lose a sense of time.*

*However, I couldn't figure out how to make a living from it, and my Haitian parents didn't encourage me to take my career in that direction. If you have Caribbean parents, you know that they value traditional careers like medicine, law and engineering, and they tend to guide their children in that direction. This is mostly because these careers are thought to guarantee financial prosperity and involve intense learning."*

In the next chapter, I'm going to do a deep-dive and complete brain dump of why blogging is a powerful source of passive income. This is the reason why it's a career that can dramatically free up your life so that you can spend more quality time with your family, significant other, or pursuing your passions.

# Chapter 8: Passive Income and The Laptop Lifestyle

New York City had just gotten its first blizzard of the year. Schools closed down. The trains stopped working. ABC's Channel 7 Eyewitness news broadcasted a series of storm warnings, urging commuters to stay inside and keep warm. Walking down the street in midtown Manhattan, you could barely see the outline of the tall buildings amidst the flurry of snowflakes.

When I was younger, I remember loving Winter's first snowfall. It was somehow magical. You'd wake up in the morning and find that everything was covered with a beautiful pristine layer of fresh snow. After rushing down stairs and gobbling up breakfast, you'd bundle up with every piece of clothes you could get your hands on so that you could go out and play.

Where I grew up, there were several epic sledding hills, ice skating ponds, and even a tiny mountain that boasted a handful of skiing trails. It a small suburban town not far from Concord, Massachusetts. For those of you history buffs, that's where the first military engagements of the Revolutionary War took place.

Unfortunately, New York City was a different matter. With so many cabs, tourists, busses, and trains, those clean fluffy snowflakes quickly turn into a brown slushy mixture that coats the entire city. It feels cold, windy, and wet. No one wants to leave their house or commute to work on the subway. When winter hits, it's harsh.

I'd tell you that I was just as miserable as the rest of New York when the blizzard hit, but for the first time in my life, I wasn't. While everyone was groaning about the storm, I was spending those brutal winter weeks relaxing on a beach in Thailand. It was a paradise.

Before leaving the United States, I secured an Airbnb in Phuket, Thailand for the price of $28 per night. This price included daily cleaning, free coffee and snacks, discounts on business in the area, and best of all, I had the entire studio to myself. It was incredible! I couldn't believe it.

Every day, I'd wake up, walk down the street to a café, and spend two hours in the morning working. Usually this consisted of reading new books, journaling, and answering any urgent emails. Then, I'd spend the rest of my time sprawled out on the beach, sipping cold beer, and swimming in the warm water.

When I first arrived, I joined a gym that was a ten-minute walk from my AirBnb so that I could work out each week and stay in shape. I know that might sound crazy, but I really do enjoy lifting weights, seeing muscle gains, and doing cardio. It puts me in such a positive mood. It also is a confidence booster. The gym also had an amazing view looking over the ocean that just made me smile.

At night, there were a ton of options to choose from. If you wanted to party it up, there were tons of bars, clubs, and dance spots to check out. For a more low-key experience, there were also lots of delicious restaurants and live music venues. Lastly, there were neat fire performances on the beach, where you could just sit and listen to the waves or gaze at the stars. It was heaven.

On a more serious note, while I was in Thailand, I also worked on myself a lot. I did yoga, meditation, and spent some quality time outlining my future goals. This "self-care" and "self-examination" work paved the way for the future. It's helped me align my work more closely with my values. I've come to learn more about my natural tendencies and inclinations. In a weird way, it helped me put all of the noise on hold so that I could take some quality time to really find myself.

As I traveled throughout Thailand, I made small talk with many of the locals and other travelers. I formed a few friendships and even began to explore some of the tropical islands in the area with newfound travel buddies. After visiting Phuket, I spent some time in Bangkok and got to see many of the cool temples, neat architecture, and the opulent Grand Palace.

I gotta tell you, I was happier than I had been in a long time. I was having adventures and loving every minute of it. It was a good trip all around.

So, why am I telling you about this? Because, there is only **one reason** that I can travel, work from anywhere, and make money on auto-pilot. This freedom allows me to live life on my own terms, without having to report to a boss. That reason can be summed up in two words: passive income.

Passive income is defined as money that comes into your pocket **whether or not** you work. You could be sleeping, chilling on a beach in Thailand, or writing a novel, but you'll still be making money. It's what all those scammy infomercials promise and how you'll "make money in your sleep." Never in my wildest dreams did I think that it could ever be a real possibility. It seemed too good to be true, and I didn't trust the people who promised that kind of a lifestyle. There just wasn't something right about them.

**(Note: if you don't like math, you can skip this section and go right to "Why Blogging is So Lucrative")**

Usually, when I mention the term "passive income," the first thing that comes to mind is investment income in the form of interest, dividends, and capital appreciation. You might also think of rental income if you own real estate. In a traditional job, you will set aside savings in the form of a mutual fund, index fund, 401k, or Roth IRA to finance your retirement.

One day, you will have enough money stashed away so that you can **retire** and live off the principle and interest of your investments. You might be 65, 70, or 75, but because of your savings, you won't have to work another day in your life. As long as you live like a miser, you'll be able to last until you're 90 or 100 without another check from an employer.

This is how most people plan to create passive income, and it's the worst way to go about it. Let me explain. In order to assess the trust cost of this strategy, we need to nail down the **cost** of acquiring savings. This is going to be different for each person. It might take you 10 years to save $50,000. For another person, it might take them 15 years. This number is important because it presents the ***effort over time*** that's required to amass a particular amount of money.

Rather than looking at $50,000 as a stack of dollar bills that you can use for X, Y, and Z, view it as a measurement in time. If it took you ten years to save that amount with your salary and expenses, then it represents ten year's worth of work.

$50,000 in savings = 10 years of work

Let's take that $50,000 and assume that you put it into a basket of stocks that resembles the S&P 500. You can achieve a 10% annual return from that money. Because of dividends, appreciation, or interest, that $50,000 turns into $55,000 after one year. You can either re-invest that extra $5,000 in passive income that you earned, or you can withdraw it to fund your lifestyle expenses.

$5,000 is not enough to fund any lifestyle, let alone a husband or wife that has to take care of a family and kids. You're looking at more like $50,000 (on the low end). So let me ask you a question. Using our little "thought experiment," how much money would YOU need to earn $50,000 in passive income from your savings?

You'd need about $500,000, and this assumes a ***very generous*** 10% annual return from stocks. The high-end dividend yield or bond return is closer to 4 – 6%. On the low end, you'd be earning $20,000 in passive income from $500,000 in savings.

This is why, usually, most people who are retired also have to withdraw on their actual savings..

I don't like this strategy. I call this the "mainstream strategy." At this rate, it will take you decades before you can live off the passive income from your savings.

What if I told you that YOU could earn an extra $12,000 per year or $1,000 per month in passive income online, and it **wouldn't take you years to accumulate.**

$1,000 doesn't seem like a lot, right? Wrong!

Remember, let's measure the value of money by the **time** it takes to acquire that money. You would need $120,000 to produce $12,000 per year in passive income. How **long** would it take you to save $120,000?

Let's say that it takes you 15 years to save $120,000. That's a lot of time. Right?

However, you can produce the **SAME AMOUNT** of passive income, except it will only take you a few months of work. All you gotta do is create an online asset, like a blog, that produces $1,000 per month in passive income.

Of course, you can make much more than $1k per month in passive income online, but I use this example because $1k per month doesn't sound crazy, right? It's doable!

The great thing is that it came in on **auto-pilot.** You didn't have to do anything. There's just a little setup work upfront, and then it's off to the races!

The mentality of most entrepreneurs is to make a bunch of money and then retire at age 40. Then, they'll be able to do what they really want. They won't have to spend their time caught in the rat race. They'll **finally** be happy.

This type of thinking can lead to a lot of sacrifices, destroyed relationships, and unhappiness. It can also lead to unethical behavior and the unhealthy willingness to succeed at any cost. As young men and women, we're sold the American dream by venture capitalists and entrepreneurship magazines.

We're told to work insane hours out of the hopes of one day being able to retire rich. Like Budd Fox says in the classic 1987 movie Wall Street, *"I think that if I can make a bundle of cash before I'm thirty and get out of this racket, I'd be able to ride my motorcycle across China."*

I'm here to share with you a strategy that will allow you to earn passive income online so that you enjoy your life **now**, not later. Once you set up these systems, you'll be able to decide how you'd like to spend your time. You could decide to continue to grow your income. You could spend your time sunbathing in a tropical climate. You could even spend more time with your family or your kids. It's up to you.

### Why Blogging is So Lucrative

Let's be honest. Most bloggers **struggle** to make ends meet. In fact, I'd say that the majority of bloggers are NOT making a full-time income. They're just doing it as a hobby.

There's nothing inherently wrong with that. We all have our own hobbies. I love to fly drones and make vlogs. The weird thing is that when you do some research, you'll quickly discover that a handful of bloggers are absolutely killing it.

They're making a very good living doing what they love.

### *How can that be?*

Why is it that the "rewards" go to a select few?

Why is blogging so lucrative for **them.**

The answer is the same reason why most people have been to a gym in their lifetime, but chances are, they aren't as fit as they'd like to be.

Perseverance and training.

Simply put, most people quit way too soon. They are dabblers. They try out blogging for a month, maybe two, and then go on to other things. They don't stick with it. There isn't enough time for them to experience the rewards that this career offers.

Wanna hear something crazy?

At the time you are reading these words, I have written over 800 blog posts in my lifetime. With a war chest of 800 pieces of content online, people are continually discovering my website day in and day out. It's almost impossible for me NOT to make money.

I'm not saying you have to write that many articles. Heck, once you start making money, you can pay other people to write the blog posts for you.

All I'm saying is that you need to be willing to persevere if you'd like to earn a substantial amount of income from blogging. I know that's hard to do. It's gonna help if you have an accountability partner.

The second fatal reason that most bloggers fail to earn a full-time income from their craft boils down to one word.

Training.

All of us, myself included, are only as good as our training. Superior results comes from superior education. We all stand on the shoulders of giants who figured out "how things work" and then taught us.

Everything from your computer all the way down to your shoes were created by other people. The only reason they were able to make them for YOU, is because someone taught them how!

Someone else went through all of the headaches, setbacks, and turmoil it takes to figure out a solution. Then, they taught it to someone else. This is the core reason why human beings improve over time. We are able to work off of and add to the findings of our ancestors.

Think about how much money you've spent to get educated.

How many tax dollars went into your education?

How much did you accumulate in student loans?

Education is *expensive* because it's *valuable.*

The bloggers who earn a full-time income from their work deliberately set time aside to master this craft. Just as I did, they sought out mentors and learned how to drive traffic, build an audience, and make money.

You can do the exact same thing.

Are you ready to build a profitable business around YOUR lifestyle?

No more dreadful commutes to work. No more late, stressful, nights slaving away for a boss you can't stand. Finally, you'll be able to work from anywhere, earn dependable passive income, and most importantly, gain a renewed sense of purpose, knowing that you're working on your passion.

In 2012, I was just like you, I had seen the online success stories and was wondering whether or not this was something that I could actually do to earn a healthy income. Late at night, I wondered what it would be like write blog posts for a living.

I could work from wherever I wanted, whenever I wanted.

I could get paid for doing what I loved... writing!

I wouldn't have to put up with an annoying boss and stupid corporate inefficiencies.

Most of all, the promise of making six or even seven figures online was too appealing to ignore. At that time, I had NO IDEA whether or not this blogging thing would really work. I kind of doubted myself, to be honest.

Like... a lot of doubt.

I didn't know anything at all when it came to "online marketing." I had no money to spend on fancy advertisements or any kind of equipment.

But, I did have one thing. I had the desire to do better in my life. For once, I decided that I was going to take action, no matter what happened.

I might be a laughingstock among my friends. I might waste my time on something silly. But, I was going to at least try.

The potential rewards far outweighed the risks!

This is the moment that I went "all-in" and committed myself to becoming a professional full-time blogger. It wasn't easy. There were many failures and stumbling blocks along the way. I learned a lot of difficult lessons.

But, it was all worth it. Two years later in 2014, I finally realized my dream. For the first time in my life, I earned $30,000 from my blog.

I felt like I was rich. It was more money than I had ever made in my life, and what's more, it was all from doing something I loved.

The next year, I earned $50,000.

I started to see more and more people becoming interested in my work. I was cited in many major media publications, like Forbes, CNN, The Wall Street Journal, The New York Times, and more.

I'm happy to share with you that last month I earned more revenue than my entire first year in 2013. Crazy, huh?

Now... you might be thinking... *"well, that's all great for you, Sal, but what about me??"*

Oh man. I wish I had a mentor when I was getting started. It would have changed my life. I would have succeeded so much faster.

You know what?! I just wish that I had someone I could trust and that would help me along the path. That's what I really wanted.

As I've become older, I've cared less and less about making money and more about building a legacy. I want to impact the world for the positive.

**Today, I'm here to share with you what was NEVER shared with me.**

A **step-by-step proven framework** that you can use to start, grow, and monetize your blog.

This is the **exact** process that I used to grow a blog from 0 to more than 20,000 subscribers.

I'm going to reveal the remarkably effective tactics I've used to get more than **2 million visitors** to my website. I'm sharing everything with you. You just have to copy it!

Take note, because this moment is literally going to transform your entire life.

As you go through the program, you're going to gain more and more clarity about how these blogging "superstars" are able to command so much attention online.

You'll discover the tested and verified principles that every professional blogger uses to get consistent traffic.

I'll hold your hand every step of the way and demonstrate these lessons with **my own** online assets. I'll give you a look behind the scenes.

There are a lot of programs online that "teach you how to do things," but I'm not **only** a teacher. I talk the talk and I **walk the walk.**

In this course, I show you how to apply these strategies to YOUR blog, but I'll also reveal how they work on my own websites. I'm talking numbers. Traffic data, income, all that.

It's time to get started. It's time to turn your passion into profit and build a thriving online business that you can be proud of.

You can join the waitlist below.

(http://www.salvadorbriggman.com/waitlist)

P.S. As a bonus, I'm giving you access to my long-awaited "passive income system."

# Chapter 9: Conclusion

I've been there...

It took me several years to build up enough courage to finally put myself out there online.

I was so nervous. Literally, I was paralyzed by fear.

What if people didn't like me?

What if everyone hated my work?

I was even embarrassed to share my early ventures with friends on Facebook. I thought they'd laugh at me and tell me that I was dreaming.

There are so many forces conspiring to keep you down in this world. So much of it is in your own mind.

You delude yourself and make "rationalizations" about how you'll get to the project in a few months and that NOW isn't the right time.

These sickening halfhearted attempts are the ENEMY of progress. They will waste years and years of your potential and effort.

Oh man, I wish I had started my blog SO MUCH SOONER. Overall, it wasn't as big a deal as I thought. All the fear was in my mind. I now get comments every day about how helpful my blog posts are.

Sometimes... we all just need that little push in the right direction.

This is my gift to you. It's time to finally time to take action!

I hope that you've enjoyed reading this book as much as I have writing it. As a brother (or sister) on the path, I wish you luck with your new plans and goals.

It would mean the world to me if you took the time to **write me a simple review** on Amazon. That would help a lot with my mission to educate about blogging :-).

Finally, if you want to drop me a line, you can tell me more about your blogging plans.

(http://www.salvadorbriggman.com/contact/)

Happy Blogging!

Salvador Briggman

*"I learned many great lessons from my father, not the least of which was that you can fail at what you don't want, so you might as well take a chance on doing what you love." - Jim Carrey*

**About the Author**

Salvador Briggman teaches writers and authors how to create a full-time income online. He has written five books, which are available on Amazon, and has started multiple successful blogs. In addition to making a living from his writing, he also hosts a popular podcast and runs a growing YouTube channel. His work has been cited by the New York Times, The Wallstreet Journal, CNN, and more.

www.ingramcontent.com/pod-product-compliance
Lightning Source LLC
Chambersburg PA
CBHW031436210526
45464CB00005B/2230